Orthodox Feasts of Christ

Also by Hugh Wybrew and published by SPCK:
Orthodox Lent, Holy Week and Easter: Liturgical Texts with Commentary

ORTHODOX FEASTS OF CHRIST AND MARY

LITURGICAL TEXTS WITH COMMENTARY

Hugh Wybrew

First published in Great Britain 1997
Society for Promoting Christian Knowledge
Holy Trinity Church
Marylebone Road
London NW1 4DU

Biblical quotations are taken from *The New Revised Standard
Version of the Bible* © 1989.

British Library Cataloguing-in-Publication Data

A catalogue record of this book is available from
the British Library

ISBN 0–281–05032–5

Typeset by Wilmaset Ltd, Birkenhead, Wirral
Printed in Great Britain by
The Cromwell Press, Melksham, Wiltshire

CONTENTS

INTRODUCTION

In all churches which follow the traditional liturgical
calendar the Christian year is shaped by two principal
cycles of festivals. There is the Easter cycle, determined by
the lunar calendar. At its heart is the celebration of the death
and resurrection of Jesus in Holy Week and at Easter. Before
Easter is the fast of Lent, after Easter come the fifty days of
Eastertide, including the Ascension of Christ, and culminat-
ing in Pentecost, the celebration of the coming of the Holy
Spirit. To these the West has added Trinity Sunday, and in
the Roman Catholic Church, the feast of Corpus Christi.

The second cycle is the one whose focus is Christmas, the
celebration of the birth of Jesus Christ. It includes the
Annunciation, the Epiphany, and the Presentation of
Christ in the Temple. This cycle celebrates significant
events in the life of Christ before his crucifixion. Still
more, it celebrates the faith of the Nicene Creed, that Jesus
Christ is 'the only Son of God, eternally begotten of the
Father, God from God, Light from Light, true God from true
God, begotten, not made, of one Being with the Father'.

This cycle to some extent overlaps with a third, that of
the festivals of the Blessed Virgin Mary. The Annunciation,
and the Presentation of Christ when called the Purification
of the Blessed Virgin Mary, link up with the Birth of Mary,
her Presentation in the Temple, and her Assumption, or
Dormition. They form a cycle of feasts of the Virgin which
are linked theologically with the Christmas cycle. For the
Creed goes on to affirm of the only Son of God that 'For us
and for our salvation he came down from heaven; by the
power of the Holy Spirit he became incarnate of the Virgin
Mary, and was made man.' Mary is celebrated for her part in
the incarnation. Linked with the first two cycles theologically, though independent in date, is the Transfiguration of

1

Christ. Celebrated in both East and West on 6 August, in Western calendars the Transfiguration also finds a place in Lent, on the second Sunday in the Roman Catholic lectionary and on the fourth Sunday in the alternative calendar of the Church of England.

Not all these festivals have equal importance in East and West. The Transfiguration is a great festival in the East; in the West it has always been of lesser importance, though it is coming to be better appreciated now. The Conception of the Blessed Virgin Mary became of major significance in the Roman Catholic Church; it is a simple commemoration in the East. The Presentation of Mary in the Temple, important in the East, has dwindled in the modern Roman Catholic calendar to a minor commemoration, because of its apocryphal origin.

In the churches of the Reformation these liturgical feasts have had varying fortunes. Some churches abolished virtually all of them. Others pruned quite severely the calendar they inherited. In the sixteenth century the Church of England abolished the feasts of the Assumption, the Conception, the Birth, and the Entry into the Temple of the Blessed Virgin Mary. The Transfiguration also disappeared. More recently, reformed calendars have tended to be enhanced, while the Roman calendar has been pruned. So the Church of England added the Transfiguration, and the Conception and Nativity of Mary, to the calendar in the 1928 Proposed Prayer Book. Other Anglican Provinces have included 15 August as the principal celebration of Mary. The Alternative Service Book's calendar in 1980 declined to do likewise. On the specious grounds that most people were on holiday in August, it gave that privilege to 8 September. But from 1998 the calendar of the Church of England will include the traditional date as a principal celebration of the Blessed Virgin Mary, a distinction it will share as a biblical red-letter day with 31 May, the Visit of the Blessed Virgin Mary to Elizabeth.

The calendar of the Orthodox Church has not been subject to modern revision, and the liturgical texts for the feasts of Christ and his Mother have remained the same for many centuries. They offer a rich contrast to the liturgical material provided for all these commemorations in the Western Churches. That provision is largely biblical. There are scripture readings and psalms chosen for their appropriateness, suitable prayers, and proper prefaces for the eucharistic prayer. There may also be brief sentences or antiphons. Further material may be added, in the form of ancient or modern hymnody. It is usually the latter which provides some kind of explicit doctrinal content to the celebration, supplementing scriptural narrative.

The liturgical material provided in the Orthodox Church for the celebration of these festivals is more extensive, and more doctrinally explicit, than that of the Western Churches. It belongs almost entirely to Vespers and Matins, and consists of hymns which both recount the story of the event commemorated, and celebrate its doctrinal meaning. This includes its significance for the worshipper; for, as the Letter to the Hebrews says, 'Since, therefore, the children share flesh and blood, he himself likewise shared the same things, so that he might ... free those who all their lives were held in slavery by the fear of death.' What happens to Jesus Christ in his humanity is meant also to happen to us.

So the Feasts of the Birth, Epiphany, Presentation and Transfiguration of Jesus Christ have direct bearing on us as believers, for they celebrate realities into which we can enter. A famous saying of the early Christian theologians, or Fathers, was that 'God became human so that human beings might become divine'. In patristic tradition the incarnation can seem to have a significance of its own, and sometimes the impression is given that we are saved by the incarnation. This theological emphasis is reflected in the Orthodox liturgical texts. But of course the incarnation can never be separated theologically from the cross: the One who

3

was born was born to die, and it was by his dying and rising again that we are saved, and have access to the divine life. But it is no less important that the One who died was in fact the Son of God, the Second Person of the Trinity, who for us and for our salvation lived the life and died the death of a human being. The incarnation is for the sake of the cross and resurrection.

This book follows *Orthodox Lent, Holy Week and Easter*, which provided a selection of liturgical texts for that season. Like its predecessor, this book has two aims. The first is to enable Western Christians to savour something of the wealth of Orthodox liturgical hymnody, with its interweaving of biblical and doctrinal themes. The second is to provide material which might be of help to them in meditating on the mysteries of the incarnation at the various festivals which celebrate God's coming among us as a human being to heal and save his creation. The texts will probably be of most value in personal prayer; but they can also be used helpfully in such contexts as the prayers after the Third Collect in Anglican Morning or Evening Prayer.

The feasts selected for inclusion in this book are the fixed feasts of the Orthodox calendar. They do not, therefore, include Good Friday, Easter or Ascension. The first two were included in *Orthodox Lent, Holy Week and Easter*; the Ascension, it is hoped, will be included in a third book, covering the fifty days of Easter, Pentecost, All Saints' Day, and selected saints' days. Nor do they include the Triumph of the Cross on 14 September, although it is one of great feasts of the Lord in the Orthodox calendar, since its themes are included in those of Lent and Holy Week.

The liturgical texts for all the fixed feasts in the Orthodox Church are contained in twelve books, one for each month, called the *Menaia*, the Books of the Month. The complete texts for the feasts of Christ and his Mother are most conveniently available, in the United Kingdom, in *The Festal Menaion*, translated by Mother Mary and Bishop Kallistos

Ware, and published by Faber. I have included for the sake of interest the commemoration of the parents of Mary, Joachim and Anna, not included in that book. As in *Orthodox Lent, Holy Week and Easter*, I have made fresh translations in modern English, almost always from the Greek, occasionally, when a text was different and seemed to me worth including, from the Romanian. From the beginning Francis Warner, Lord White Fellow in English Literature at St Peter's College, Oxford, who helped me greatly with the translations of the earlier book, has been kind enough to take a keen interest in this new selection, and I am much indebted to him for his suggestions for improving the translations, and his encouragement in pursuing the project. I have again used the New Revised Standard Version of the Bible for scriptural phrases or allusions.

There is a brief account of the development of the fixed feasts in Chapter 1, to provide the background and context of the liturgical texts. To each main section there is an introduction, and each concludes with a theological and spiritual commentary.

NOTES

Since this book is intended primarily for Western readers, titles of feasts have been given in chapter headings in their Western form. The Orthodox titles have been given in the introductory chapter on the development of the calendar, and are used, in shortened form, in the subheadings in each chapter.

Mary's title, affirmed by the third ecumenical council of Ephesus in 431, is in Greek 'Theotokos'. Because it is not easy to translate accurately and concisely, it is often simply transliterated. This is perhaps not entirely satisfactory for Western readers, and can seem rather exotic. Although it means strictly God's birthgiver, I have preferred to use the term Mother of God, more familiar to Western ears. It is a term which exists also in Greek, alongside Theotokos: icons of the Virgin are usually inscribed *Meter Theou*, Mother of God.

1 THE DEVELOPMENT OF THE CHRISTIAN YEAR

Feasts of Christ

For the first three centuries of the Church's life, there was only one festival in the year apart from Sunday, the weekly commemoration and celebration of Christ's resurrection. That was Easter, the Christian passover, celebrated according to the lunar calendar inherited from Judaism. In the course of the fourth century that celebration came to be spread over the eight days from Palm Sunday to Easter Day. It was preceded by a fast of varying length, and followed by the fifty days which were concluded by Pentecost, or Whitsunday. The only other commemorations were those of the martyrs. From the end of the second century, the anniversary of the martyr's death, or heavenly birth, was celebrated at the tomb, over which churches often came later to be built.

It was early in the fourth century that the fixed feasts, those celebrated according to the solar calendar, began to find their way into Christian liturgical observance. The first was the celebration of Christ's birth or appearing, on 25 December in the West, and on 6 January in the East. There is clear evidence of this celebration by the fourth decade of the century. By the end of the fifth century the feasts of Christ with which we are concerned in this book, Christmas, Epiphany, Presentation and Transfiguration, had all made their appearance, even if they were not yet all universally observed.

THE PERSON OF JESUS CHRIST

These feasts of Christ were introduced into the fixed calendar at the same time as the Church was coming to a clearer mind about how to express its faith in the person of Jesus Christ.

7

That process of elucidation was carried forward by the general, or ecumenical, councils of the Church, chiefly in the fourth and fifth cenuries, but continuing until the seventh and eighth. It was the product of controversy in the Church about two aspects of Christian belief: the relationship of Jesus Christ to God the Father, and the person of Jesus Christ himself, as both human and divine. It is necessary to say something about the development of the Church's doctrine concerning both these aspects of its faith, since the dogmatic formulations which were eventually accepted by the greater part of the Church were soon reflected in liturgical texts. This was particularly the case in the Eastern part of the Church, where the doctrinal controversies originated, and where the councils met which tried to resolve them.

DOCTRINE OF GOD AS TRINITY

Early in the fourth century heated controversy broke out about the relationship of Jesus Christ to God the Father. In Alexandria the presbyter Arius taught that the Son was inferior to the Father, the highest of all creatures, but nevertheless a creature. He quoted Scripture in defence of his teaching. He was opposed by Athanasius, deacon and later bishop of the church in Alexandria, who insisted that Jesus Christ was equal with the Father. Again, he could quote other scriptural passages to back his argument. The controversy threatened to divide the Church, which the Emperor Constantine had decided to sponsor as a unifying force in his vast empire. It was his decision to call a council of all the bishops of the empire to resolve the dispute. The council, later to be recognized as the first ecumenical council, met in Nicaea in 325, under the Emperor's chairmanship. It decided against Arius, and to safeguard the Church's belief adopted the Greek word *homoousios* to describe Jesus Christ, the Son of God, in his relation with the Father. The Son is 'of one substance', or 'one in being' with the Father. He is God in the same way the

Father is God, consubstantial and coeternal with the Father. The Council of Nicaea approved a statement of faith, a creed, which formed the basis of the so-called Nicene Creed. That creed was in fact the work of the second ecumenical Council of Constantinople, which in 381 affirmed that the Holy Spirit is also consubstantial and coeternal with the Father and the Son. So in the course of the fourth century the Church's doctrine of God as Trinity was elucidated, in the heat of often bitter controversy.

DOCTRINE OF THE PERSON OF JESUS CHRIST

Discussion and debate moved on in the fifth century to the person of Jesus Christ. He had clearly been a human being. But the Church's faith also proclaimed him to be one of the three Persons of the Trinity. How could one person be both divine and human? Several explanations were proposed and held by different church leaders and their followers. At the extremes, one view emphasized his divinity in a way that seemed to others to diminish or even abolish his real humanity; another sought to affirm his full humanity in a way which others saw as undermining the unity of his person, setting a human Jesus alongside the divine Son. These two approaches were associated respectively with the theological schools of Alexandria and Antioch.

Two ecumenical councils in the fifth century attempted to resolve this controversy, which raged no less fiercely, among ordinary people as well as among theologians, than the dispute over Arianism had done. In 431 the Council of Ephesus affirmed the validity of calling Mary 'Theotokos', Mother of God, against those, including Nestorius, Archbishop of Constantinople, who held she should be called Mother of Christ. It was a title, the Council held, which defended the divinity of Jesus Christ, and the unity of his person, against the more extreme form of Antiochene teaching. The Council of Chalcedon in 451 affirmed, contrary to the more extreme form of

Alexandrian doctrine, that Jesus Christ is one person in two natures, divine and human. It produced what is known as the Chalcedonian definition, which proclaimed:

> We all with one voice confess our Lord Jesus Christ one and the same Son, the same perfect in Godhead, the same perfect in manhood, truly God and truly man, of a rational soul and body, co-essential with the Father according to the God-head and co-essential with us according to the manhood ... to be acknowledged in two natures, without confusion, without mutation, without division, without separation, the distinction of natures being by no means taken away by the union, but rather the property of each nature being preserved and concurring in one person and one hypostasis.

The doctrinal definitions of these councils were accepted by the majority of churches. Some of them were not acceptable to all, and divisions resulted in the Eastern part of the Church which are still not healed, although in recent years a great measure of doctrinal agreement has been reached between the Churches which accepted them, and those which did not.

Feasts of Mary

The feasts of Mary began to make their way into the calendar about a century later, and appear in the course of the fifth and sixth centuries, perhaps even later in the case of the Annunciation. The latter is now regarded in the West as a feast of Christ, and its full modern Roman title is the Annunciation of Our Lord to the Blessed Virgin Mary. Like the three feasts of Christ mentioned above, its theme is rooted in the gospel narratives. That distinguishes it from the other feasts of Mary, which have no basis in the New Testament. They are concerned with incidents described in Christian writings, dating from the second to the fourth centuries, which are included in what is conventionally, if rather misleadingly, called the Apocryphal New Testament. It is necessary to say something about them, since they are the source, both of the imagery of the liturgical texts for these feasts, and of their iconography as well.

APOCRYPHAL MARIAN WRITINGS

Two of these writings are of interest to us, so far as this book is concerned. They are the *Protevangelium of James*, and the *Assumption of the Virgin*. They can be found most conveniently in *The Apocryphal New Testament*, edited by J. K. Elliott, and published by the Clarendon Press, Oxford. The origin of the former is now usually dated to the second half of the second century, that of the latter to the fourth century. They were written to cater for widespread interest among Christians in details of Mary's life to which no reference at all is made in the New Testament. The *Protevangelium of James* tells of the miraculous birth of Mary, and her early years, until her betrothal to Joseph. It then tells the story of the annunciation and birth of Jesus, based on Luke's account, and of the visit of the wise men, from Matthew's. The evangelical accounts are expanded and embroidered, in order to highlight the miraculous character of Jesus' birth, and the virginity of Mary after, as well as before, she gave birth. The *Assumption of the Virgin* tells of her death, and its miraculous circumstances, and recounts how Christ bore her soul to heaven, and how her body was raised up on the third day.

These apocryphal writings clearly responded to a powerful religious need among Christians, particularly in the East, where they seem to have originated. They circulated in all parts of the Church, in a variety of languages, and in different versions. Since they were not Holy Scripture, they could the more easily be adapted to suit the religious views of the copyist or translator. The *Protevangelium of James* was discouraged in the West after the time of Jerome, in the late fourth century, because it made Joseph the father of several children by a previous marriage. Jerome thought the 'brothers and sisters of Jesus' were cousins, a view still officially taught by Rome.

The historical value of these writings is almost certainly minimal. They were composed to satisfy popular religious needs, and to promote beliefs about Mary which began to be held quite early on, although entirely without biblical foundation. But they passed into the tradition of the Church, and had an important influence on the development of Marian doctrine. Through their contribution to liturgical and iconogaphic traditions, they became an integral part of Eastern Orthodoxy.

But it is important to note that, despite the exaltation of Mary in the doctrine and devotion of East and West alike, a difference emerged between the two traditions. In the East Mary was never venerated for herself alone, but always as the Mother of the incarnate Son of God; and she was never separated from the Church, of which she is the figure. In the West, medieval and Counter-Reformation developments in Mariology and Marian devotion tended to distinguish her from the Church, and exalt her in her own right. Popular Eastern devotion to Mary has of course often done the same: strict doctrine has not always controlled popular devotion in the way theologians might wish.

Doctrine and Worship

The doctrinal controversies and definitions about God as Trinity and the person of Jesus Christ as truly God and fully human had a significant impact on Christian liturgical worship, especially in the East. Opposing parties within the Church made use of popular songs to propagate their beliefs among ordinary Christians. These were not at first necessarily liturgical songs. But doctrine soon came to exercise an extensive influence on liturgical texts. The formula 'Glory be to the Father and to the Son and to the Holy Spirit, as it was in the beginning, is now and ever shall be' was invented to express orthodox trinitarian doctrine, and replaced the older formula, 'Glory be to the Father through the Son in the Holy Spirit', which was capable of an Arian interpretation. The phrase 'Christ our true God', frequently used in those Eastern Churches which accepted the Council of Chalcedon, gave liturgical expression both to the faith of the Council of Nicaea, that the Son of God Jesus Christ is equal to the Father, and also to the faith defended by the Council of Chalcedon, that the single person of Jesus Christ was both human and divine – the faith expressed by Mary's title of 'Mother of God'. The hymns which came to be written for liturgical feasts of Christ and for those of his Mother were heavily influenced in their language and imagery by the doctrine affirmed by the councils. The titles of the feasts, too, with their stress on Jesus Christ as 'our Lord and God and Saviour', and on Mary as 'Mother of God', reflect the mature theology of the East. The West tended to be more conservative in its liturgical language, and continued in general to refer to the Father as God, to whom the Church prays through Jesus Christ and in the Holy Spirit.

No less influential in the development of the liturgical tradition were the apocryphal Marian writings, and the beliefs they both reflected and propagated. While Mary's title Mother of God had conciliar authority, doctrines such as the perpetual virginity of Mary were first spread rather as popular beliefs. But they were equally given liturgical expression: among the adjectives always associated with the mention of Mary in Orthodox texts is 'ever-virgin'. The *Protevangelium of James* is the first known text to uphold the notion that Mary retained her virginity after as well as before the birth of Jesus Christ.

The influence of doctrine on worship is abundantly evident in the texts given in subsequent chapters of this book. In the Orthodox Church liturgical worship is one of the most important vehicles of doctrinal teaching. Orthodoxy has always restricted dogma to a minimum: most of its teaching is contained in texts meant for use in worship. Conversely, the corporate prayer of the Church, which liturgical worship is, has been shaped by doctrine to a greater extent in the East than in the West. Doctrine shapes and informs prayer; prayer brings doctrine to life.

Anticipation and Prolongation of Feasts

Already in late fourth-century Jerusalem the celebration of the major feasts lasted for eight days. This was so in the case of Epiphany, Easter and the Dedication Festival (known as Encaenia) of the Martyrium, Constantine's great church on Golgotha, and of the Church of the Resurrection, the rotunda built by his son over the tomb of Christ. In time octaves, as these eight-day celebrations were called, came to be attached to all the most important feasts in the Western Calendar. In the East feasts came to be prolonged by a varying number of days, constituting the 'afterfeast'. At the same time, the East developed the custom of preparing for major festivals by a varying number of days before the feast itself, the 'forefeast'. Christmas seems to have been the first of the fixed feasts to have acquired such a preparatory period: by the end of the ninth or beginning of the tenth century Christmas troparia were used from 22 December onwards.

In time, too, appropriate commemorations came to follow some of the major festivals. The earliest may have been the commemoration of Mary on 26 December. That had certainly found a place in the calendar of Constantinople by the end of the ninth century; and so had the commemoration of Mary's parents, Joachim and Anna, on 9 September, that of John the Baptist on 7 January, and that of Simeon and Anna on 3 February. The commemoration of the Archangel Gabriel on 26 March was added later.

The Twelve Great Feasts

Eventually twelve feasts of Christ and his Mother came to be recognized as great festivals in the Orthodox Church. These rank after Easter, which is the feast of feasts, and so not included in the twelve. They are, in calendrical order, the Birth of the Mother of God, the Exaltation of the Cross, the Entry into the Temple of the Mother of God, Christmas, Epiphany, the Presentation of Christ, Annunciation, Palm Sunday, Ascension, Pentecost, the Transfiguration, and the Dormition. The Twelve Great Feasts celebrate the incarnation, passion and glorification of God the Son, and the main events in the life of his Mother, inseparable from the incarnation of God in her Son. Within the twelve, the feasts of Christ rank higher than those of his Mother: when they occur on a Sunday their texts replace completely those of the Sunday, while the texts for feasts of Mary are combined with them. The icons of these feasts form a sequence in the second row of an iconostasis, though the sequence of icons does not always correspond exactly with that of the feasts in the calendar, and varying sequences of icons are found.

Feasts of Christ and His Mother

So the development of the Church's calendar from the fourth century onwards took place under the influence of the formation of Christian doctrine, and of the burgeoning traditions about Mary which found expression in apocryphal New Testament writings. It will perhaps be helpful to say something here about the history of the individual feasts whose liturgical texts form the principal subject matter of the following chapters. They are given in the order in which they occur in the calendar, beginning with the Birth of the Blessed Virgin Mary, since the Orthodox liturgical year, following Byzantine practice, still begins on 1 September.

BIRTH OF THE BLESSED VIRGIN MARY
8 September

This celebration began in Jerusalem, and was in origin the dedication festival of the church built by the Sheep Pool, or Pool of Bethesda, by the mid-fifth century, and dedicated to St Mary. By the ninth century tradition had located the house of St Anna, Mary's mother, close by. The festival was adopted in Constantinople in the sixth century, when Romanos the Melodist composed hymns for it, some of which are still used. From the East its celebration spread westwards, and it entered the calendar of the Roman Church, probably during the pontificate of Sergius I (687–701), who came from Antioch in Syria.

The full title of the feast in the Orthodox Church is The Birth of our Most Holy Lady the Mother of God. It is preceded by a forefeast of one day, and is continued during four days of afterfeast. September 9 is observed as the commemoration of Mary's parents, Sts Ioachim and Anna, the holy and righteous ancestors of God.

PRESENTATION OF THE BLESSED VIRGIN MARY
21 November

This feast commemorates Mary's presentation in the Jerusalem temple when she was three years old. Like the celebration of the birth of Mary, this too has its origin in Jerusalem, with the dedication in 543 of the 'New Church of St Mary, Mother of God', built by the Emperor Justinian. By the seventh century it was generally observed in the East, and was adopted in Rome as well at the end of the century.

Its full Orthodox title is The Entry into the Temple of the Most Holy Mother of God. It is preceded by a forefeast of one day, and followed by four days of afterfeast.

CHRISTMAS
25 December

The observance of 25 December as the celebration of the birth of Christ first appeared in the West. Its first mention is in a Roman calendar for the year 336. The date may have been chosen as a deliberate counter to the pagan observance on 25 December of the feast of the Unconquered Sun, instituted in the third century on what had by then come to be accepted as the winter solstice. From Rome it spread to other parts of the West, and to the East, where 6 January had become the date of a similar celebration of the Epiphany, or manifestation, of Christ. Constantinople adopted it in 379, Antioch in 386. In time both dates came to be observed in East and West alike, although in Jerusalem it was only in the sixth century that 25 December was finally admitted to the calendar, when the Emperor Justin II (565–578) ordered its observance throughout the empire.

Christmas was the liturgical celebration of the doctrinal definition of the first ecumenical Council of Nicaea in 325, which affirmed Jesus Christ as the Son of God to be 'of one substance', or 'one in being', with the Father.

In the Orthodox Church Christmas is preceded by a fast of forty days. From 1 December the coming of Christ is an increasingly prominent theme in the liturgy. On the second Sunday before Christmas the holy ancestors of Christ are commemorated, beginning with Adam and including Abraham, Isaac and Jacob, David, and the Old Testament prophets who foretold Christ's coming. On the Sunday before Christmas are commemorated all the righteous, from Adam to Joseph, the husband of Mary, including many commemorated the previous Sunday, and many others too. There are five days of forefeast, beginning on 20 December, and on 24 December, the Eve of Christmas, the so-called Royal Hours are celebrated. They are the usual Hours, from the First to the Ninth Hours, with the addition of scripture readings, and Vespers on the Eve is followed by the Liturgy of St Basil. The Vigil consists of Great Compline followed by Matins. There are six days of afterfeast, lasting until 31 December. December 26 is kept as a feast of Mary, called the Synaxis of the Mother of God – perhaps the earliest of the feasts of Mary. (Synaxis literally means 'assembly', and came to denote a feast on which Christians gathered to commemorate a saint associated with the previous day's feast.) The full Orthodox title of Christmas is The Birth according to the Flesh of our Lord and God and Saviour Jesus Christ.

(All the Orthodox Churches keep Christmas on 25 December. But some, including the Russian and Serbian Orthodox Churches, still follow the Julian calendar, which is now thirteen days behind the Gregorian calendar. This means that those churches keep old-style 25 December on new-style 7 January. Since the Orthodox liturgical day begins on the previous evening, Christmas celebrations begin with Vespers on 24 December. When the old calendar is used, that falls on 6 January according to the new. This has led to a popular but mistaken view that the Orthodox Church celebrates Christmas on 6 January.)

EPIPHANY
6 January

The Epiphany is one of the oldest feasts in the Christian calendar. It originated in the East, where the date was believed to be the winter solstice. It was a celebration of all the manifestations of Christ in the world, including his birth and his baptism. When 25 December came to be celebrated as well, as the feast of the birth of Christ, to which in the East was attached also the visit of the Magi, 6 January came to be the celebration of his baptism.

The Orthodox Church refers to it as the Theophany, the manifestation of God on earth: in full The Holy Theophany of our Lord and God and Saviour Jesus Christ. As one of the great feasts of the Lord, it is preceded by four days of forefeast. Like Christmas, its immediate preparation is an Eve, whose liturgical observance consists of the Royal Hours. It is followed by eight days of afterfeast, of which the first, 7 January, is the Synaxis of the Honoured and Glorious Prophet, Precursor and Baptist John.

An important feature of the Epiphany in the Orthodox Church is the Great Blessing of the Waters, which takes place at the end of the Liturgy of St Basil the Great, celebrated after Vespers on the Eve of the feast. The custom of blessing water on this day, on which water was sanctified by Christ's baptism, goes back at least to the fifth century. This origin of this custom was originally independent of the baptism of new Christians, although the practice of baptizing at Epiphany goes back to the end of the fourth century. By the sixth century an association had come to be made between the two in some places, but not everywhere. In Constantinople about AD 900 water was blessed in the Church of the Holy Wisdom on the Eve of Epiphany, and then the water of the font was blessed in preparation for baptism next morning.

PRESENTATION OF CHRIST
2 February

This is another of the festivals which originated in Jerusalem. It was in the calendar by 383, when Egeria, a monastic pilgrim from the West, was in the holy city, and wrote a description of its liturgical observances for the benefit of her sisters at home. She gives it no specific name, but says it is the commemoration of the fortieth day after Epiphany, the manifestation of Christ. Since at that time 6 January was the only celebration of the appearing of Jesus, the fortieth day fell on 14 February. The feast was adopted in Constantinople in the mid-sixth century, perhaps in connection with the fifth ecumenical council. The council met in the capital in 553, and had the doctrine of the person of Jesus Christ on its agenda. By then 25 December had been adopted in Constantinople alongside 6 January, and so the feast was celebrated on 2 February. In the course of the sixth and seventh centuries, its observance spread throughout the Church in East and West.

There was some uncertainty about its status as a feast of Christ or of Mary, and this is reflected in the various names given to it. The Presentation of Christ, the Purification of the Blessed Virgin Mary, the Meeting of Christ, are titles found both in East and West. The Purification of the Blessed Virgin Mary became the standard title in the West, until the reformed Roman Missal of 1970, when the feast was called The Presentation of Christ – a title already used in the Church of England's Book of Common Prayer of 1662.

In the East the feast soon came to be called The Meeting, that is, of the incarnate Son of God with his people, so making it clear that it is a feast of the Lord. Its full title is The Meeting of Our Lord and God and Saviour Jesus Christ. In the Orthodox calendar it has one day of forefeast, and seven days of afterfeast, though these can be curtailed if they would fall wholly or in part in Lent or the preceding week. The day after the feast is the commemoration of Sts Simeon and Anna.

ANNUNCIATION
25 March

The first mention in the East of the Annunciation as a liturgical festival is in 692, in one of the canons of the Council 'in Trullo', held in Constantinople. This canon allowed the feast, which usually occurs in Lent, to be kept with a celebration of the Eucharist, as though it were a Saturday or Sunday – there is no eucharistic celebration on the weekdays of Lent in the Orthodox Church. There is a reference to it in Rome at about the same time, during the pontificate of Sergius I, who introduced the feast of the Birth of Mary to the Roman calendar. Although as a feast its introduction may have been relatively late, the date of 25 March was very early associated with the conception as well as the death of Jesus, and it may have been from this date that the date of Christmas was determined. Earlier, the Annunciation was commemorated on the first or second Sunday before Christmas. In the West it is now the theme of the last Sunday in Advent.

The Annunciation of the Most Holy Mother of God and Ever-Virgin Mary, to give it its full Orthodox title, has one day of forefeast, and is followed on 26 March by the Synaxis of the Archangel Gabriel. It has no afterfeast, since it falls always either in Lent or in Easter Week. Western practice does not allow the Annunciation to be celebrated either in Holy Week or in Easter Week, but transfers it to the Monday of the second week of Easter. But in the Orthodox Church it is always celebrated on its proper day, even if that falls on Good Friday, Holy Saturday or Easter itself. Its services are combined with those of the day, in accordance with extremely complicated rules, which provide for all possible combinations of the feast itself with other major liturgical days falling about that time.

TRANSFIGURATION
6 August

The liturgical celebration of the transfiguration probably originated in the dedication of churches built in the fifth century on Mount Tabor to commemorate the event. From Palestine the feast spread rapidly thoughout the East, where it was general by the end of the first millennium. It spread more slowly in the West, and became general only in 1457. But it never had the same status in the West as in the East, where it became one of the great festivals of Christ.

The full title of the feast in the Orthodox Church is The Transfiguration of Our Lord and God and Saviour Jesus Christ. As one of the great feasts of the Lord, it has one day of forefeast, and seven days of afterfeast.

ASSUMPTION
15 August

The cult of Mary developed rapidly after her proclamation as Theotokos, or Birthgiver of God, by the third ecumenical council at Ephesus in 431. By the middle of the fifth century there was a commemoration of Mary as Theotokos at the second mile from Bethlehem, where in the *Protevangelium of James* she is said to have rested half-way between Jerusalem and Bethlehem on her way to give birth to Jesus. A church had been built there in the time of Patriarch Juvenal of Jerusalem (425–458). At the end of the century the celebration was transferred to a church built over the tomb of Mary in Gethsemane. It was there that the celebration was linked with the death of the Mother of God, called her Dormition, or falling asleep. (In the East it is generally held that Mary died, and then was raised to the life of heaven: hence the term Dormition, indicating her death. In the West, it came to be widely held that she did not die, but was taken up body and soul into heaven: hence the term Assumption. But the latter does not exclude the possibility of her dying before she was taken into glory.)

The feast was extended to the whole of the Byzantine Empire at the end of the sixth century, perhaps in connection with a foundation made by the Emperor Maurice (582–603) next to the church in Gethsemane. At the same time he ordered the observance to be held only on 15 August, probably the date of the dedication of a church in Mary's honour: up till then 18 January was an alternative date for the celebration, linking it with the Epiphany.

The Dormition, or Falling Asleep, of Our Most Holy Lady

the Mother of God, to give it its full Orthodox title, is one of the great feasts of the calendar. It has one day of forefeast, and eight days of afterfeast.

2 Birth of the Blessed Virgin Mary

The New Testament says nothing about the early life of Jesus' Mother. But in the Church's tradition, Mary, like other significant people in the history of Israel, was born by the direct intervention of God. According to the second-century *Protevangelium of James*, her parents, Joachim and Anna, were righteous but childless. Once when Joachim, a rich man, went to the temple to offer his gifts to the Lord, he was not allowed to do so, because he had not raised up offspring in Israel. Saddened by this rejection, he researched to see whether all the righteous in Israel had had children. He found they all had, including Abraham, to whom God gave a son in his old age. With him in mind, Joachim went into the wilderness, saying nothing to his wife, and fasted with prayer for forty days.

His wife Anna, too, mourned her childlessness and her presumed widowhood. At the prompting of her maid Judith, just before the great day of the Lord, she exchanged her mourning for bridal clothes, and sat down under a laurel tree in her garden. Remembering Sarah, she lamented that she was barren, and prayed to God for a child. An angel of the Lord appeared to her, and told her that her prayer had been heard. She would conceive and give birth to a child, whose fame would spread throughout the world. Anna promised that any child she bore would be given to the Lord and serve him all its life. Two angels told her that her husband was on his way, and had been told by an angel of the Lord that his wife would conceive.

Meanwhile an angel of the Lord had appeared to Joachim, too, and told him his prayer also had been heard. His wife would conceive. He took lambs, calves and goats from his flocks as an offering to the Lord, on his own behalf and on that of the priests and elders, and all the people, and went back to Jerusalem. Anna was standing at the gate, and when she saw him coming she ran and embraced him, and said 'Now I know that the Lord God has greatly blessed me; for behold the widow is no longer a widow, and I, who was childless, shall conceive.'

Joachim offered his gifts the next day, and knew, from the appearance of the priest's frontlet – an oracular plate – when he took his gift to the altar, that he had been forgiven and justified. In due time Anna gave birth to a baby girl, and named her Mary.

The themes of the texts for the feast of the birth of Mary are largely derived from this story in the *Protevangelium of James*. They run through the services of each of the three days from which texts are given here: the Forefeast of the Birth of the Mother of God on 7 September, the Birth of the Mother of God on 8 September, and the commemoration of righteous Joachim and Anna on 9 September. The language in which these themes are presented is that of the fully-developed doctrine of the incarnation, formulated by the third and fourth ecumenical councils, of Ephesus in 431 and Chalcedon in 451.

The icon of the feast is reminiscent of that of the birth of Jesus Christ. Anna is depicted lying on a couch, with attendants nearby, while one or two maids wash the new-born child in a basin. The infant is also shown, wrapped in swathing bands and lying on a small couch next to Anna's bed. Sometimes she is depicted in a cradle, rocked by another maid. From a window Joachim looks down on the scene.

Forefeast of the Birth of the Mother of God
7 September

FROM VESPERS

The spiritual beams
of the whole world's rejoicing,

have shone upon the lands
at your birth, pure Lady,
foretelling to all
the Sun of glory,
Christ our God.
For you have shown yourself
mediator of true rejoicing
and of grace.

Your worshipful birth,
most pure and holy Virgin,
heaven's angelic hosts
and human race on earth
combine to praise.
For you became Mother
of Christ our God,
the creator of all.
We pray you, intercede
incessantly with him for us,
who, next to God,
in you have placed our hopes,
Mother of God unwedded
and highly praised.

Marvel most glorious!
From barren mother
and childless father,
from righteous Joachim and Anna,
the branch that flowers
today gives birth
to the Mother of God,
innocent of marriage.
The prophets' fellowship,
the patriarchs' company,
rejoice at your birth.

From the root of Jesse
and from David's loins,
God's daughter Mary
is born to us today.
So all things rejoice,
and are made new,
heaven and earth unite in joy.
Praise her, all generations.
Joachim rejoices, Anna celebrates.
She cries out:
The barren gives birth
to the Mother of God,
and our life's sustenance.

FROM MATINS

In marvellous fashion
from barren womb
were you born:
beyond nature's way
from maiden loins
you gave birth.
Beautiful shoot,
you put forth
life for the world.
So the heavenly powers
cry out to you,
Mother of God:
Glory, holy Lady,
to your coming!
glory to your virginity!
glory to your birthgiving!
For you alone are most pure.

Today, by God's counsel,
Mary the Virgin

and Mother of God,
the heavenly bridegroom's
holy bridal chamber,
is born of the barren,
that she might become
the vehicle of God's Word.
For to this end
was she marked out beforehand
as gate of divinity
and true life's Mother.

On the barren
is fruit bestowed,
Mary, God's daughter.
Her the divine prophets
foresaw in the Spirit.
Today we who see her
leap in Anna's bosom,
let us join trusting Joachim
at the spiritual banquet;
and invite those
who are far off, saying:
Now is the world's summons,
for from barren womb
has sprung forth God's gate
and true life's Mother.

Exult, all creation,
with sensations of joy;
for of devout Anna,
who is called Grace,
and godly Joachim,
is born beyond hope
Mary most pure,
and chaste Mother of God.
Her offspring became

humankind's salvation:
Christ our God
of her become human,
in way beyond telling.

Birth of the Mother of God
8 September

FROM VESPERS

Today God who rests
on spiritual thrones
has prepared himself
a holy throne on earth.
He who in wisdom
fixed the heavens,
in love for humanity
a living heaven
for himself has made.
From a fruitless root
he has made to grow
a life-bearing branch:
his Mother.
God of marvels,
hope of the hopeless,
Lord, glory to you!

What sound is this
of those who revel?
Joachim and Anna
hold mystic feast and say:
Adam and Eve,
rejoice with us today.
For to us who long ago,
by breach of the commandment,

shut ourselves out of Paradise
most noble fruit is given,
God's daughter Mary:
she opens for us all
the way back in.

Come, all we who believe,
make haste to the Virgin.
There is born the one ordained,
before she was conceived,
to be Mother of our God.
There is born
virginity's treasure,
Aaron's sprouting rod
from the root of Jesse,
the prophets' proclamation,
righteous Joachim and Anna's offspring.
So she is born,
and by her birth
the world is made new.
She is born,
and the Church is arrayed
in her beauty:
she, the holy temple,
divinity's vessel,
virginal engine,
royal nuptial chamber,
wherein came to pass
the marvellous mystery
of the union beyond telling
of the natures come together
in Christ; whom we worship,
and praise the birth
of the Virgin all-blameless.

FROM MATINS

From Jesse's root
and David's loins
to us today is born
God's daughter Mary.
All things are renewed,
engodded all things.
Heaven and earth,
rejoice together;
families of the nations,
praise her.
Joachim rejoices,
Anna celebrates
and cries out:
The barren gives birth
to the Mother of God
and our life's nourishment.

Joachim and Anna
from childlessness' disgrace,
Adam and Eve
from death's decay,
were set free, pure Lady,
by your holy birth.
That birth your people celebrate,
from guilt of sins redeemed,
as to you they cry out:
The barren gives birth
to the Mother of God
and our life's nourishment.

You contained in your womb,
Virgin Mother,
one of the Trinity,
Christ the king.
All creation praises him,

before him quake the heavenly hosts.
Pray to him,
Lady most honoured,
to save us.

The death that came on humankind
by eating from a tree
has been destroyed
by the Cross today.
The curse afflicting humankind,
of our first mother Eve,
has been undone
by the offspring
of God's pure Mother.
All the heavenly powers
extol her.

Adam, be renewed!
Eve, be extolled!
Prophets, dance for joy
with the apostles
and the upright!
Angels and men
share one joy in the world.
Today of the upright,
Joachim and Anna,
is born God's Mother.

Marvel extolled!
The source of life
is born of one barren;
grace begins to bear glorious fruit.
Rejoice, Joachim,
for you are father
of the Mother of God.
No other earthly father

is like you, blessed by God.
For through you
has been given us
the Virgin who contained God,
the divine dwelling-place,
the holy mountain.

Joachim and Anna's prayers and sighings
for their barren childlessness
were heard, acceptable, by the Lord;
and they brought forth for the world
life-giving offspring.
He prayed on the mountain,
she in the garden suffered from her shame.
But with joy the barren
gives birth to the Mother of God
and our life's nourishment.

Commemoration of Sts Joachim and Anna

9 September

FROM VESPERS

All creation today rejoices,
illustrious Mother of God,
and with one mind celebrates
the yearly memory of your parents,
wondrous Joachim and Anna.
For they brought joy to all,
beyond all hope
giving birth to you,
from whom has shone forth
the Light
and our life's nourishment.

Anna today rejoices,
in spirit exulting,
and rejoicing is glad,
succeeding at last
in bearing a child,
so long desired.
For she has brought forth
the divine fruit
of promise and blessing,
Mary, all without blemish;
who gave birth to our God,
and caused the Sun to shine
on those who sat in darkness.

Blessed couple!
You surpass all parents,
for you have brought forth
her who excels all creation.
Truly blessed are you, Joachim,
such a daughter's father named.
Blessed is your womb, Anna,
for you have given birth
to our life's Mother.
Blessed your breasts,
which have suckled
her whose milk nourished
the nourishment of all.
We pray you, blessed ones,
intercede with him for us
to save our souls.

FROM MATINS

From the root of Jesse
has sprung up a shoot,
whence a branch has blossomed,

filling all mankind
with the sweet scent
of divinity.

Rejoice now, Anna,
set free from barren bonds,
and nourish the Pure One.
Summon all to praise him
who has given to mortals
from her womb
the only Mother
who knows no husband.

She who was freed
through prayer
from childless bonds
summons us with her
to celebrate the marvel,
and bring gifts to her
who is born,
and leap and dance
with longing before her,
as once the maidens
ran speedily forth,
dancing and crying out:
Here is the summons to all!
Look, Adam is set free,
for Anna has born a child,
the only Mother
who knows no husband.

Today the Pure One,
all without blemish,
comes forth from the barren.
Today all things rejoice
at her coming to birth.

> Adam is loosed from his bonds,
> Eve is set free from her curse.
> All heavenly things rejoice,
> on mankind peace is bestowed.
> We cry out, giving praise:
> Glory to God in the highest heaven,
> and on earth peace
> among those whom he favours!

The *Protevangelium of James* was written to satisfy the demands of piety and exalt the person of Mary. Although it has no canonical status, it became widely read and accepted, especially in the Eastern part of the Church. The author was perhaps inspired by instances of miraculous births in the Old Testament, such as those of Samson (Judges 13) and Samuel (1 Samuel 1); a more immediate model may have been that of the annunciation and conception of John the Baptist in St Luke's Gospel (Luke 1.5–25). He emphasizes the significance of Mary by presenting her birth, like theirs, as the consequence of a direct intervention of God himself.

That intervention, as the liturgical texts make clear, was part of the divine plan for saving creation. Mary's birth came as a climax of the work of God among his chosen people. From the beginning God had been working towards the incarnation of his Son in Jesus. The prophets of Israel were among the few who saw what God was doing; and they were understood by the Church to have foretold, not only the birth of Jesus as the Christ, but also the birth of his mother Mary. She was predestined by God for her particular role in his coming into the world to save it.

So if the texts glorify Mary, they do so as Mother of the Messiah, of Jesus the Christ, the Second Person of the Trinity become human in her. She is exalted, not for herself, but for her free and glad obedience to the saving will of God. Her title, Mother of God, was given her by the Council of Ephesus to safeguard the reality of the incarnation: it was God who became human, so that human beings might become divine. The liturgical texts always venerate Mary as the Mother of her Son.

The Birth of the Mother of God is the first major festival of the Orthodox calendar. It is a feast of the incarnation, for it is the first intimation of what will be celebrated in its fullness at Christmas, with the birth of her Son. Leaving aside the apocryphal nature of the story on which they are based, its texts can be used for meditation on the providence of God, working throughout human history, and especially the history of Israel. They serve, too, to remind us that God works within human history only with human co-operation freely given. They remind us, finally, that the scope of God's salvation is not less than cosmic: it is not just humankind, but the whole of creation that is to be taken into God, to share in his life.

3 Presentation of the Blessed Virgin Mary

The incident itself, and the details of the story, are found in the *Protevangelium of James*. Anna had promised that any child she had would be brought as a gift to the Lord, and serve him all the days of its life. So when Mary was two, Joachim proposed she should be taken up to the temple. Anna thought it better to wait until she was three, and would miss her parents less. So they waited another year.

Then the undefiled daughters of the Hebrews were summoned, and told to take a burning torch each, to capture Mary's imagination and prevent her being tempted to turn back from the temple. The high priest Zechariah welcomed her and blessed her, and told her that the Lord had magnified her name among all generations, and that because of her the Lord at the end of the days would reveal his redemption to the children of Israel. He placed her on the third step of the altar. God gave her grace, she danced, and was beloved of all Israel. She showed no sign of wanting to go home with her parents when they left. Fed miraculously by an angel, she stayed in the temple until she was twelve. Then an angel of the Lord told Zechariah to betroth Mary to one of the widowers in Israel, whom the Lord would indicate.

It is this apocryphal story which provides the themes of the hymns both of the forefeast and the feast itself. As with the texts celebrating the birth of the Mother of God, so with these: their language is informed by the fully developed doctrine of the incarnation of the fifth century. This celebration is closer to Christmas than that of September; and this is reflected in the use of some of the hymns for 25 December in the canon at Matins on 21 November.

The icon of the feast depicts the story told in the *Protevangelium*. At the door of the temple, at the top of some steps, stands the prophet Zechariah in priest's robes. He holds out his hands, like Simeon in the icon of the presentation of Christ, to receive the three-year old child. She goes up the steps towards him, carrying a lamp in one hand, and holding out the other. Her parents are behind her, looking at each other and pointing to Mary. A group of virgins carrying lamps is nearby. The icon combines this image of the entry itself with another of Mary seated high up above the temple beneath a canopy. She takes the bread brought by the archangel Gabriel, who blesses her.

Forefeast of the Entry of the Mother of God into the Temple
20 November

FROM VESPERS

Torch-bearing virgins
joyfully accompany her
who is always a virgin.
They foretell in the Spirit
of a truth what will happen.
For the Mother of God,
the temple of God,
as a child is led
with virgin glory
to the temple.

Today the temple
of God's dwelling,
the Mother of God,
is brought into the Lord's temple
and Zechariah welcomes her.
Today the most holy place rejoices,
and the angelic host

keeps mystic festival.
We too celebrate with them today,
and with Gabriel we cry out:
Greetings, favoured one!
The Lord is with you,
who has abundant mercy.

Come, all believers,
and praise her who alone
is without blemish,
whom the prophets foretold,
who was brought into the temple.
From all eternity
she was predestined
to be Mother,
and in these last times
she has been revealed
as Mother of God.
Lord, by her prayers
give us your peace
and abundant mercy.

FROM MATINS

God's temple,
the priceless marriage chamber,
with shining torches
and in merry mood
comes before to be brought
to the temple of God.
Zechariah rejoices over her,
as he sees clearly
the prophets' company
begin already to escort her.
Joyfully he cries out to her:
Your arrival in advance,

maid and virgin mother,
discloses joy to come.

The Maker of all things,
Creator and Lord,
stooped down
in pity untold
and in love for humankind;
when he saw fallen
the work of his own hands,
he took pity on us
and willed to raise us up,
by a more divine creation
and by emptying himself,
for by nature he is
good and merciful.
So he took Mary,
a virgin and pure,
to be the mediator
of the mystery,
of whom he took our nature,
as he freely willed.
She is the tent of heaven.

Heaven above, rejoice today!
Clouds, rain down joyfulness!
because of the mighty works,
most marvellous,
of our God.
For the gate which faces east,
born by promise
of a barren childless mother,
and hallowed for God's abode,
is brought today into the temple
as a sacrificial offering
without blemish.

David, rejoice
and pluck your harp,
for he says:
Behind her the virgins
shall be led to the king,
her companions shall be led along.
Within, in God's tent,
inside his place of atonement,
she will be brought up
to be his abode,
who was eternally begotten
of the Father,
without change,
for our salvation.

Entry of the Mother of God into the Temple

21 November

FROM VESPERS

Today the living temple
of the holy glory,
of Christ our God,
alone among women
blessed and pure,
is brought as an offering
into the law's temple,
to live in the sanctuary.
With her rejoice in spirit
Joachim and Anna.
The chorus of virgins
sing to the Lord with psalms,
and honour his Mother.

Into the holy of holies
the holy and spotless one

is brought in the Holy Spirit
to make her home there.
By an angel is fed
the one who is truly
the most holy temple
of our holy God,
who has made all things holy
by her entrance,
and has made divine
fallen human nature.

After you were born,
divine Bride and Lady,
you went to the Lord's temple,
to be brought up,
yourself holy,
in the holy of holies.
Then Gabriel was sent to you,
spotless as you were,
to bring you food.
All in heaven were astonished,
when they saw the Holy Spirit
make his home in you.
So, Mother of God,
pure and spotless,
praised in earth and heaven,
save our human race.

A joyful day has dawned,
an illustrious festival.
For today is brought into the temple
the one who was virgin
before childbirth,
and remained virgin
after childbirth.
Old Zechariah,

the Precursor's father,
is glad and in joy cries out:
The hope of the afflicted
has come to the holy temple,
herself holy,
to be sanctified
as a dwelling for the king of all.
Let Joachim the ancestor be glad,
and let Anna rejoice,
for they have brought to the Lord,
like a three-year old heifer,
the spotless Lady.
Mothers, rejoice with them;
virgins, leap for joy;
barren, be glad with them.
For the one foreordained
to be Queen of all
has opened for us
the kingdom of heaven.
Be merry and joyful,
all you peoples.

FROM MATINS

Before you were conceived,
Pure Lady,
you were dedicated to God;
now you have been born on earth,
you have been brought to him,
a gift fulfilling your parents' promise.
Truly yourself temple of God,
you have been brought into God's temple,
pure from childhood,
with bright lights;
you have been revealed
as Light's abode,

God's own inaccessible Light.
Truly great is your entry,
you who alone are God's bride
and always a virgin.

The Saviour's most pure temple,
priceless wedding chamber and Virgin,
the holy treasure house of God's glory:
she is brought today
into the Lord's house,
bringing with her
the divine Spirit's grace.
God's angels praise her:
She is the tent of heaven.

I rejoice as I see the grace
of God's hidden mysteries
revealed and plainly fulfilled
in the Virgin.
I am at a loss to know
how I should understand
the hidden fashion strange
in which the undefiled one
has been revealed as alone chosen
beyond all creation,
seen and unseen.
So my mind and tongue
are gripped by fear
when I want to praise her.
Yet I am bold
to proclaim and extol her:
She is the tent of heaven.

Announced long ago
by the prophets' company
as jar (of manna),

(Aaron's) staff,
(Covenant's) stone tablet,
mountain from which
no stone's been cut:
praise we Mary,
God's daughter,
with faith.
For today she is brought
into the most holy place,
to be brought up for the Lord.

Nourished in faith, O Virgin,
with heavenly bread
in the Lord's temple,
you brought into the world
the Bread of life,
the Word of God.
To him you were betrothed
beforehand by the Spirit
in mystic fashion,
a temple chosen
and without blemish;
and you became the Bride
of God and the Father.

Mary was born in accordance with God's providence and his plan for the salvation of the human race. The feast of the Entry of Mary into the temple represents the next stage in the divine preparation for the incarnation of the Second Person of the Trinity in Jesus the Christ. She was born in order to give birth to the divine Word. Dedicated to the Lord before her conception, she is now presented in the temple, to live a life of total self-offering to God. The historicity of the event is doubtful, but its liturgical commemoration can be understood as primarily theological: Mary is being prepared in the temple to become herself the temple of the living God. The texts speak of her being betrothed to God the Word, and becoming the bride of God the Father.

Here, as always in Christian reflection about her, Mary is not to be separated from the Church of which she is a figure. The New Testament applies to the Church what these texts say of Mary. St Paul says that Christians are the temple of God, in which God's Spirit dwells. Like Mary, the Church is a holy temple where God lives in the Spirit (1 Corinthians 3.16–17). The Church, too, is the bride of Christ. Again it is St Paul who writes: 'I promised you in marriage to one husband, to present you as a chaste virgin to Christ' (2 Corinthians 11.2). The Revelation to John takes up the same theme, when the visionary sees 'the holy city, the new Jerusalem, coming down out of heaven from God, prepared as a bride adorned for her husband' (Revelation 21.2). The Church, like Mary, is called by God to bring Christ into the world, to embody in its own life the love which God is, and which was fully embodied in the human life of Jesus.

As we reflect on the dedication of Mary to God's loving purpose, symbolized by her presentation in the temple and her life there, we are reminded that the Christian community, and each member of it, is called to a life of no less dedication. For us as for Mary, this celebration encapsulates Paul's appeal in Romans 12.1, 'I appeal to you, therefore, brothers and sisters, by the mercies of God, to present your bodies as a living sacrifice, holy and acceptable to God, which is your spiritual worship.' The Spirit is with us, as he was with Mary, to enable us to become dedicated temples of God's presence, and to bring forth divine love in the world.

4 CHRISTMAS

Christmas is the feast next in importance to Easter, both in the East and West. It commemorates the birth of Jesus. Vespers on the evening of 24 December includes prophetic readings from the Old Testament. Among them is part of the story of creation from Genesis 1, and the prophecy of Daniel about the stone cut from the mountain, which destroyed the great image (Daniel 2.31–36, 44–45). There are also passages more familiar to Western Christians as prophecies of Christ's coming, including the prophecy of the star coming out of Jacob (Numbers 24.17–18), the ruler from Bethlehem (Micah 5.2), and the rod from the stem of Jesse (Isaiah 11.1).

When Christmas falls on a weekday, Vespers is followed by the Liturgy, at which the readings are Hebrews 1.1–12, used in the Roman and Anglican lectionaries at the Christmas morning Eucharist, and Luke 2.1–20, the story of the birth, the angels and the shepherds, used at the Midnight Mass in the Western tradition. At the Liturgy on Christmas morning the readings are Galatians 4.4–7, about God's Son being sent forth so that we might receive adoption as sons and daughters, and Matthew 2.1–12, the visit of the three Magi, reserved in the West for Epiphany.

From these scripture readings come most of the themes of the hymns for the Christmas services. They are interwoven with other scriptural allusions, and permeated by the doctrinal affirmations about the person of Jesus Christ and his Mother made in the course of the fourth and fifth centuries. The story of the creation in Genesis provides the background for the theme of the new creation in Christ, and the renewal of humanity in the image and likeness of God. Throughout the texts, it is the doctrinal note which is dominant: the various strands of the story subserve the basic theme of the incarnation. Christmas is the celebration of God become human, so

48

that humanity might become divine.

That is reflected by a curious feature of the Liturgy on Christmas Day. Instead of the Trisagion, a chant sung before the scripture readings, these words from St Paul's letter to the Galatians are sung: 'As many of you as were baptized into Christ have clothed yourselves with Christ. Alleluia' (Galatians 3.27). This chant is usually used on festivals with which baptism was once connected. Although Christmas was not one of these, its use today emphasizes our own rebirth in Christ as an important aspect of the celebration of Christ's birth.

The icon of the feast depicts in one image episodes which in the Gospels are separate. Mary is shown lying on a couch, with the infant Jesus wrapped in swaddling bands beside her, in a manger often resembling a small coffin. Sometimes she is looking at him, sometimes away from him. Gazing reflectively at the child are an ox and an ass, which come from Isaiah 1.3 rather than the gospel narrative. Above, a star shines. Below in the composition two midwives prepare to give the child his first bath, while on the other side Joseph sits on a rock, looking usually rather disconsolate, as though he did not quite believe what had happened, while an old man wearing a shepherd's cloak talks with him. The angels above sing glory, the shepherds marvel, while in the distance the three Magi can be seen, already making their way to worship Christ.

Forefeast of the Birth of Our Lord Jesus Christ
24 December

FROM VESPERS

Rightminded
make we hymns resound
on the forefeast
of Christ's birth.

For he who is honoured
with Father and Spirit
in his compassion
puts on our nature,
and comes to be born
in Bethlehem's town.
The shepherds with angels
praise his birth
beyond telling.

All peoples,
let us celebrate in advance
the feast of Christ's birth.
Lifting our minds to Bethlehem,
let us go there in thought,
and see in the cave
the great mystery.
For Eden stands open
as from a pure Virgin comes God,
perfect in his divinity,
perfect in his humanity.
So cry we out:
Holy God, eternal Father;
Holy Mighty, incarnate Son;
Holy Immortal, advocate Spirit;
Trinity Holy, glory to you!

Listen, heaven,
pay attention, earth.
For the Son and Word
of God and the Father
comes to be born
of a young girl
who has known no man,
by his goodwill,
who impassibly begot him,

and by the Holy Spirit's co-operation.
Bethlehem, prepare yourself;
open your gate, Eden.
For the one who eternally is
becomes what he was not,
and all creation's shaper
himself takes human shape.
So he bestows on his world
abundant mercy.

Once in Bethlehem
there was registered,
with the old man Joseph,
David's descendant Mary.
She was carrying a child
conceived without seed.
Her time had come to give birth,
and there was no room in the inn.
Yet the cave turned out
to be a delightful palace
for the Queen.
Christ is born
to raise up the image
which before was fallen.

FROM MATINS

The prophets' words are now fulfilled;
for tomorrow our God is born
of the Virgin Mary
in manner beyond telling,
yet remains what he was
before he was born.
The Magi come together
to bring him gifts;
the shepherds spend the night

in the fields;
we too sing praise:
Lord, you have been born
of a Virgin,
glory to you!

How shall I not marvel
at the Virgin who gives birth,
at the star which tells
of the one who is born,
at the child wrapped
in bands of cloth,
at the Magi who kneel
with gifts before him?
I see too the poor manger,
and the angels around it,
praising with hymns
the Lord of all and crying:
Glory to God in the highest heaven,
who willed to be born a young child,
and is God from all eternity.

He who dwells in unapproachable light,
and holds all things together,
in his inexpressible compassion
is born of a Virgin;
as a child is he wrapped
in bands of cloth,
and in a cave
is laid in cattle's manger.
Speed we to Bethlehem
to worship him
with the Magi,
and to bring as our gifts
the fruit of good works.

Bethlehem, welcome God's Mother,
for she has come to you
to bring forth the inaccessible light.
Angels, marvel in heaven;
men and women, give glory on earth;
Magi from Persia,
bring your triple gift.
Shepherds, by night
keeping watch in the fields,
sing the threefold holy hymn.
Let everything that breathes
praise the Creator of all!

Birth of Our Lord Jesus Christ
25 December

FROM VESPERS

Come and rejoice in the Lord,
while we tell of the mystery we celebrate.
The dividing wall is broken down;
the flaming sword draws back;
the cherubim leave open
the way to the tree of life.
I taste of the sweetness of Paradise,
from which I was expelled
because of my disobedience.
For the exact image of the Father,
the imprint of his eternity,
takes the form of a slave,
coming forth from a Mother
who knows no marriage,
and suffering no change.
For he has remained what he was,
true God;

and he has taken upon himself
what he was not,
becoming human for love of humanity.
To him let us call out:
You have been born of a Virgin:
O God, have mercy on us.

What shall we bring you, O Christ?
For our sake you showed yourself
on earth as a human being.
Each of the creatures you have made
brings you thanks:
the angels, song;
the heavens a star;
the Magi, gifts;
the shepherds, wonder;
the earth, a cave;
the desert, a manger;
while we bring a Virgin Mother.
O God, you are before all ages,
have mercy on us.

When Augustus became sole ruler on earth,
the multitude of human dominions
came to an end.
When you became incarnate of the pure Virgin,
the multitude of idols
came falling down.
The cities came under a single worldly authority,
and the nations believed in a single divine kingdom.
The peoples were registered by Caesar's decree;
and we who believe have been registered
in the name of your divinity,
of our God who has become human.
Great is your mercy, O Lord,
glory to you!

FROM GREAT COMPLINE

Heaven and earth today are met,
since Christ is born.
Today God has come down to earth
and humankind gone up to heaven.
Today he who in his own nature
cannot be seen,
for humans' sake
is seen in human body.
Let us then praise him
and cry out:
Glory to God in highest heaven,
and on earth peace,
which your coming, Saviour,
has given us.
Glory to you!

When Jesus saw humankind,
made in God's image and likeness,
fallen by disobedience to the commandment,
he bowed the heavens and came down,
and made his abode in a virgin womb,
without change, so that there
he might remake corrupt Adam,
who cries out:
Glory to your appearing,
my rescuer and my God.

Your birth, O Christ,
has caused the light of knowledge
to shine upon the world;
for by it those who revered the stars
have learned by a star to worship you,
the Sun of righteousness,
and to know you,

the dawn from on high.
Lord, glory to you!

FROM MATINS

Why, Mary, do you marvel?
Why are you astounded
at what is in you?
Because, says the Virgin,
I have borne in time the eternal Son,
and I do not know
how the child was conceived.
I have no husband:
how should I bear a Son?
A birth without seed,
who has ever seen?
But where God wills,
as it is written,
nature's order is overcome.
Christ has been born of the Virgin
in Bethlehem of Judaea.

He who has nowhere been contained,
how is he contained in a womb?
He who is in the Father's bosom,
how lies he in his Mother's arms?
Yes, it has all happened
as he knew,
as he willed
as he wished it to be.
For, bodiless,
he willed to be embodied;
and he who is,
for us became what he was not;
without losing his own nature,
he shared the substance of ours.

In two natures is Christ born,
for he wished to fill the world above.

The Virgin today gives birth
to him who is above being;
the earth gives a cave
to the unapproachable.
Angels with shepherds praise,
wise men travel by a star.
For a young child is born for us,
who is God before all ages.

Today in Bethlehem
Christ is born of a Virgin.
Today begins to be
the one who has no beginning:
and the Word of God becomes human.
The heavenly powers rejoice,
earth with humankind makes merry.
The wise men bring gifts;
the shepherds tell the wonder;
and we cease not to cry:
Glory to God in highest heaven,
and on earth peace
among those whom he favours!

In Eastern Christian tradition Christmas is a celebration of
salvation, no less than Easter. The doctrines of God as Trinity
and Jesus Christ as truly both human and divine were not
elaborated as academic exercises. They were formulated to
defend the Christian experience of new life through the death
and resurrection of Jesus; for in Jesus God was working to
reconcile the world to himself. If it was not God himself
working in Jesus, then we are not saved, for only God can save
us.

So the texts of Christmas celebrate the light of divinity

revealed in the birth of Jesus, and marvel at the wonder of the transcendent God who becomes one of his own creatures. All the stress is on the God who becomes human. This reflects the doctrinal approach of the fourth- and fifth-century councils, for whom the starting point was faith in Jesus as the divine Word, the Second Person of the Trinity. The Word unites human nature to himself in Jesus. But Jesus Christ, the incarnate Word, is not a human person: the person of Jesus is the person of God the Son, who has become human, without ceasing to be divine, in the womb of Mary.

So there is less emphasis on the birth of the human Jesus in the Orthodox celebration of Christmas than there has come to be in the Western. The Christmas crib, first used by St Francis of Assisi, has no place in the Orthodox tradition. There is here some contrast between the Orthodox and Western approaches to Christmas. Some Western Christians might be surprised by the emphasis on the divinity of Jesus; for much modern Western thinking about Jesus begins from the fact that he was a human being, and then goes on to ask in what sense he might be God. The Orthodox texts exactly reflect the dogmatic tradition of the ecumenical councils, which began from the divine, and then asked how God might also be human.

Christmas in the Orthodox tradition is essentially a celebration of the incarnation of God in Jesus. The birth of Jesus is the fruit of God's own initiative, by which he enters the world as one of his own creatures. He does so in order to overcome the separation of humankind from its creator, caused by human sin. The Word of God becomes human, to bring the light of truth to those who live in ignorance, to free from condemnation those who share in the guilt of Adam's fall. So humankind, and all creation, is reconciled to God, and shares in the life and joy of heaven. 'God became human so that human beings might become divine' was a theological slogan of the fourth and fifth centuries, which expresses both the divine initiative, and also its saving purpose.

The hymns of Christmas often reflect that slogan, in speaking almost as though salvation were achieved by the incarnation alone; and we have already seen similar language in connection with the birth and entry into the temple of Mary, in preparation for the incarnation. They contain few references to the death of Jesus and the victory of the cross. One such reference is found in one of the hymns for 26 December, and understands the three gifts of the Magi as symbolizing Jesus' three days in the tomb. Some Western carols, too, link Christ's birth to his death. But the incarnation cannot of course be understood as effecting salvation by itself, apart from the death and resurrection of the incarnate Lord. The New Testament is clear that it is the cross which frees us from sin, reconciles us to God, and renews our human nature. The Christmas texts must be understood in this light: they read back into the birth of Jesus the consequences of his death and resurrection.

Christmas is as much a celebration of our rebirth as it is of the birth of Jesus. The renewal of human nature is a theme which runs through the hymns for these days. Nor is it only humanity which is renewed: the whole of creation is made new, and so joins with humankind in rejoicing at the birth of Jesus, the Word become human.

Synaxis of the Mother of God
26 December

The Synaxis of the Mother of God on 26 December may be the earliest commemoration of Mary. It seems likely that before there was any specific day set aside for her commemoration in the calendar, she was eulogized in sermons in connection with Christmas. There was no liturgical cult of Mary in the first three centuries. The first evidence for such a cult comes from Arabia in the fourth century, when women inaugurated an annual festival, at which special cakes called *collyrides* were offered to the Virgin Mother. Her commemoration at Christmas time is obviously appropriate, and became customary before the particular feasts of Mary began to be introduced into the calendar.

In iconography Mary is normally depicted with Jesus Christ: icons of her alone are much less frequent. She is shown holding Christ on one arm. Sometimes she points to him with her free hand, at others she holds him to her with it. Though of small size, the representation of Christ shows him always with adult features, and his hand is often raised in blessing. It is a mother-and-child image, and yet it has none of the naturalistic human qualities of many Western versions of this theme. For this is an icon of the incarnation: Mary is the Mother of God, and her Son is the incarnate Word of the Father.

FROM VESPERS

All things were enlightened
when the Lord Jesus was born
of the holy Virgin.
Shepherds watched in the fields,
and Magi worshipped,
angels sang praise,
Herod was disturbed.
For God our Saviour
has appeared in flesh.

Your kingdom, Christ our God,
is an everlasting kingdom,
and your sovereignty
is from generation to generation.
You took flesh of the Holy Spirit
and became human of Mary ever Virgin.
So you shed light on us,

Christ our God,
by your coming.
Light from light,
the Father's reflection,
you have made all creation
glow with joy.
Everything that breathes
praises you, the exact imprint
of the Father's glory.
O God, you are and you were,
and you have shone out
from a Virgin:
have mercy on us.

Lord, you have come to Bethlehem,
and have made a cave your home.
You have been laid in a manger,
whose throne is heaven.
You have come to be with shepherds,
whom hosts of angels surround.
And all this,
in your heart's goodness,
to save our race.
Glory to you!

How shall I proclaim
so great a mystery?
He is embodied
who has no body;
the Word takes solid form;
the invisible is seen;
the untouchable is touched;
he who is without beginning
begins to be.
The Son of God
becomes son of man,

Jesus Christ, the same
yesterday and today and for ever.

FROM MATINS

He who was born
before the morning star
of the Father without mother,
is today without father
incarnate on earth of you.
So a star tells the good news
to the Magi,
and angels with shepherds
praise, favoured one,
your pure childbirth.

The mystic vine bore
the untrodden bunch of grapes,
bearing it in her arms
like a branch, and said:
You are my fruit,
you are my life.
From you, my God,
I have come to know
that I am what I was.
For now that I see
my virginity's seal undamaged,
I proclaim you to be
the immutable Word,
become embodied.
I knew no seed:
but I know you to be
corruption's destroyer.
For though you came out of me,
I remain pure;
you have left my womb

as you found it.
So all creation with me rejoices,
and to me it calls out:
Hail, favoured one!

Come, let us praise in song
the Saviour's Mother,
who after childbirth
is seen still a virgin.
Rejoice, living city
of our king and our God,
where Christ made his home
and accomplished salvation.
With Gabriel we praise you,
give you glory with shepherds;
and we cry:
Mother of God, pray to him,
who of you was incarnate,
to save us.

Today the invisible divine nature
is born of a Virgin
and united with mortal creatures.
Today in Bethlehem unbounded Being
is wrapped in bands of cloth.
Today by a star
God brings Magi to worship him,
announcing beforehand,
by gold, myrrh and incense,
his three days in the grave.
So we sing:
Christ our God,
you have become incarnate
of the Virgin:
save us!

The texts for the commemoration of the Mother of God continue the themes of Christmas Day. This makes it clear that Mary is venerated because of her part in the incarnation. She is honoured by the Church as the Mother of God the Son become human. We have seen that as early as the second century there was much interest in some Christian circles in Mary, which writings like the *Protevangelium of James* both reflected and sought to satisfy. As veneration of Mary grew in the Church, there was a tendency in popular piety to honour her for herself, and to regard her as a focus of prayer and devotion in addition, or even alternative, to her Son. But in the Church's teaching she is never separated, either from her Son, or from the Church of which she is the figure. The recovery of this perspective in Western theology in recent years owes much to the influence of Orthodoxy.

In the Orthodox iconographic tradition, an image of the Mother of God with Christ is normally placed in the semi-dome of the apse of the Church above the sanctuary and altar, and so in a deliberate relationship with the celebration of the Eucharist. As Mary brings forth Christ, the embodied love of God, into the world, so in its celebration of the Divine Liturgy the Church too, through her prayer for the coming of the Holy Spirit to make the bread and wine the body and blood of Christ, brings Christ into the world. Sharing in the Eucharist, the Church itself is taken into Christ, and so in the power of the Spirit is enabled to make the love of God embodied in him a reality in the life of the world. In Mary we contemplate a model for the Church's own vocation.

5 EPIPHANY

In the Eastern part of the Church 6 January was in origin the equivalent of the Western celebration of 25 December. Both celebrated the incarnation of God in Jesus, the manifestation of God in human form. When East and West came to keep each other's dates as well as their own, each had in effect two feasts of the incarnation, closely related. The themes of the former single celebration came to be distributed between the two dates rather differently by East and West. The West celebrated the birth of Jesus with the visit of the shepherds on 25 December, and on 6 January celebrated the visit of the wise men, or kings, as the manifestation or Epiphany of Christ to the Gentiles.

The East, as we have seen, celebrated on 25 December the birth of Christ, the visit of the shepherds, and the coming of the wise men with their gifts. Then, on 6 January, it celebrated the baptism of Christ, as the Theophany, or manifestation of God in the flesh. In the Orthodox Church Theophany has remained the title of the feast, whose full form is The Holy Theophany of Our Lord and God and Saviour Jesus Christ.

The theme of the hymns for the day is drawn from the evangelical accounts of Jesus' baptism. But the story is interpreted in the light of the Chalcedonian definition of the person of Jesus Christ: it is God become human who comes to be baptized by John; and so his descent into Jordan sanctifies its waters, and all water, including of course the water used in baptism. Traces of ancient mythology are to be found in references to Christ destroying the powers of evil which lurk in the watery depths.

The special feature of the Orthodox services for the Theophany is the Great Blessing of the Waters. This takes place at the end of the Liturgy of St Basil the Great, celebrated after Vespers on the eve of the feast. A large vessel of water is prepared in the Church. There are readings from the Old and New Testaments, followed by St Mark's account of Jesus' baptism. Then a litany for the sanctification of the water is chanted, after which the priest reads a lengthy prayer of blessing. The cross is lowered three times into the water, while the troparion of the feast, 'Your baptism in Jordan, Lord' (see below), is sung. The church and congregation are sprinkled, and all drink from the blessed water. The people take some of it home with them.

There is a second Blessing of the Waters after the Liturgy on the day of the feast itself. Where possible the clergy and people go in procession to a river, or to the sea; where this is not possible, the blessing again takes place in church, with the same order of service.

The icon of the feast depicts the gospel story. Jesus is shown standing in the river Jordan, which is sometimes personified in the figure of an old man in the water at the bottom of the icon. John the Baptist stands on one bank, while angels stand ministering on the other. At the top of the scene there is a symbol of heaven, from which the Spirit, in the form of a dove, descends in a ray of light. It denotes too the Father's voice attesting his beloved Son. The icon is understood as a trinitarian icon, since it includes representions or symbols of all three Persons of the Trinity.

Forefeast of the Theophany of Our Lord Jesus Christ

5 January

FROM VESPERS

River Jordan, prepare yourself;
for Christ our God comes
to be baptized by John,
that by his Godhead

he might shatter
in your waters
the dragons' unseen heads.
Be joyful, Jordan's desert,
mountains, leap for joy.
For Life eternal has come
to summon Adam back.
Precursor John,
cry out with the voice
of him who cries out:
Prepare the way of the Lord,
and make his paths straight.

Let Jordan's desert rejoice
and bloom like the lily.
For in it has been heard
his voice who cries:
Prepare the way of the Lord.
For the one who weighed
the mountains in scales
and the valleys in a balance,
who fills all things as God,
is baptized by a servant.
The one who gives rich gifts
begins to become poor.
Eve heard it said: In pain
you shall bring forth children.
But now the Virgin hears:
Greetings, favoured one,
the Lord is with you,
who has abundant mercy.

Jordan's river once returned,
struck by Elisha's mantle,
when Elijah ascended into heaven,
and the waters were parted,

to the one side and to the other.
For him the watery way became dry,
and so truly prefigured baptism,
by which we cross over
life's transient stream.
Christ has shown himself in the Jordan,
to make holy all water.

FROM COMPLINE

One is the grace
of the Father and of the Son
and of the Spirit,
which brings to perfection
those who in faith cherish
divine baptism's gift,
and receive the power
to become God's children
and cry out:
Blessed are you, O God.

By your strange birth
of a Virgin, Word of God,
in manner beyond nature,
we looked at you already with wonder.
But now you are glorified,
marvellously accomplishing
this great mystery,
which, through your participation,
has become the bath
where, by the divine Spirit,
many children are brought to birth.

The earth, Word of God,
has been made holy
by your holy birth:
heavens with stars

proclaimed your glory.
Now water's nature is blessed
by your bodily baptism,
and earthborn's race
has returned again
to its former high estate.

FROM MATINS

Christ, eternally reigning
with the Father and the Spirit,
now in these last times
becomes incarnate of the Virgin,
he alone knows how,
and comes to be baptized,
so bestowing immortality
on all who are washed
in the divine bath.

The one who in Bethlehem
from the Virgin shone forth
in bodily form,
to the Jordan now hurries
to wash off earthborn's defilement;
so, by divine baptism,
he brings to the light
those who sat in darkness.

John the Baptist,
you have known me
from the womb as the Lamb.
Serve me in the river,
ministering with the angels.
Holding out your hand,
touch my holy head.
When you see the mountains quake
and Jordan turning back,

cry out with them:
Glory to you, Lord,
for you became incarnate
of the Virgin,
for our salvation.

Theophany of Our Lord Jesus Christ
6 January

FROM VESPERS

When the Precursor saw our Light,
who enlightens everyone,
coming for baptism,
he rejoiced in spirit
and his hand shook.
He pointed him out,
and said to the peoples:
Look, this is he
who redeems Israel,
who frees us from decay.
Christ our God,
you are without sin,
glory to you!

When the hosts of angels
saw our Redeemer
baptized by a slave
and attested by the Spirit's coming,
they were terrified.
And a voice came from heaven,
from the Father:
This man, on whom the Precursor
lays his hand,
is my Son, the Beloved,

with whom I am well pleased.
Christ our God,
glory to you!

Jordan's waters received
you, the Source,
and the Advocate,
like a dove, descended.
He bowed his head,
who bows the heavens.
The clay cried out
to him who shaped him:
Why do you command
what is beyond me?
I need your baptism.
Christ our God,
you are without sin,
glory to you!

When you wanted to save
humankind gone astray,
you did not think it
beneath you to take
the form of a slave.
It became you,
Lord and God,
for our sake
yourself to take on
all our properties.
For your baptism, Saviour,
in human flesh
has won our forgiveness.
So we cry out to you:
Christ our God,
our Benefactor,
glory to you!

FROM THE GREAT BLESSING OF THE WATERS

The voice of the Lord
above the waters
cries out and says:
Come, all of you,
and take of the Spirit of wisdom,
the Spirit of understanding,
the Spirit of the fear of God,
of Christ who has showed himself.

Today is made holy
the nature of water;
Jordan is parted,
and holds back
its own waters' flow;
for it sees the Lord
washing himself.

As a human being
you came to the river,
Christ our king;
and without delay,
for you are good,
you received a servant's baptism
at the Precursor's hands,
because of our sins,
for you love humankind.

Your baptism in Jordan, Lord,
revealed the Trinity's worship
For the Father's voice
testified to you,
naming you his beloved Son;
and the Spirit, like a dove,
affirmed this saying true.
Christ our God,

you have shown yourself
and enlightened the world:
glory to you!

FROM GREAT COMPLINE

Christ is baptized,
and comes up from the water,
with him raising up the world.
He sees the heavens opening,
which Adam had closed
for himself and his descendants.
The Spirit attests his Godhead,
for it comes upon him
as like upon like.
A voice is heard from heaven,
for thence comes the one attested,
the Saviour of our souls.

When John saw you,
Christ our God,
coming to him
at the river Jordan,
he said: Lord,
why do you come to a servant,
since you have nothing to wash off?
In whose name shall I baptize you?
Of the Father?
But you carry him within you.
Of the Son?
But you yourself are he,
become human.
Of the Holy Spirit?
But you know you yourself
give the Spirit to believers,
by the breath of your mouth.

O God, you have appeared:
have mercy on us.

FROM MATINS

When you appeared, Saviour, in the Jordan,
and were baptized by the Precursor,
you were attested as the beloved Son.
So you were seen to be
without beginning like the Father.
The Holy Spirit came upon you.
In him we too are enlightened,
and cry out:
Glory to God who is in Trinity.

You have shown yourself
today to the whole world,
and your light, Lord,
has shone on us,
who praise you
with understanding.
Light inaccessible,
you have come
and revealed yourself.

On Galilee of the Gentiles,
on the land of Zebulun,
and the land of Naphtali,
as the prophet said,
has shone Christ,
a great light.
To those who sat in darkness
a bright light has dawned,
a lightning-flash from Bethlehem.
More truly, from Mary
has the Lord,

the Sun of righteousness,
shed his rays
over all the world
So then let us all,
naked because of Adam,
come and clothe ourselves
in him, to be warmed.
For you have come,
a cover for the naked,
and daylight for those
who sit in darkness;
light inaccessible,
you have revealed yourself.

'God is light and in him there is no darkness at all' wrote St
John in his first letter (1.5). Light is a constant theme in the
texts for the Theophany, which is sometimes called the Feast
of Lights. At the baptism of Jesus the light of God is revealed,
in order to enlighten those who live in the darkness of sin. In
the early centuries of the Church sin was sometimes understood as ignorance, and the purpose of Christ's coming was to
bring the light of the knowledge of God, and of the way we
were meant to live. So baptism was often called enlight-
enment, and those preparing for baptism were those being
enlightened. This tradition has contributed to the imagery of
the hymns for the Theophany.

The Jesus who came to John for baptism was the Word of
God, the Second Person of the Trinity. That basic truth of
Christian faith and of Chalcedonian orthodoxy is stressed
repeatedly in the texts. So he had no need himself of being
baptized: he was in every way sinless. But in Mary's womb he
had united human nature with himself, and he was washed in
the Jordan in order to purify from sin the whole of humanity.
When Jesus was baptized the power of sin was broken, and
fallen humanity, symbolized in Adam, was created anew. Nor
was it only humanity which was renewed: the whole of

creation was set free from corruption, and raised up with Christ. The gates of Paradise, closed because of Adam's sin, were opened again, so that all created beings and things might enter the kingdom of God.

The descent of Jesus into the waters of Jordan made all water holy, and gave it sanctifying power. The blessing of water at Theophany renews for us now what happened in Jordan then. The blessed water is sacramental, and brings forgiveness, healing, and spiritual power and protection to those who are sprinkled with it and drink it. Water is not blessed on this occasion with a view to baptism. But this feast was once one of the times particularly favoured for baptizing, and this theme is not absent from the celebration of Theophany. At the Liturgy the Trisagion, a chant sung before the scripture readings, is replaced by these words from St Paul's Letter to the Galatians, 'As many of you as were baptized into Christ have clothed yourselves with Christ. Alleluia' (Galatians 3.27).

The texts for the Theophany, read by themselves, imply that salvation has been achieved by the baptism of Jesus. That of course is not so: we are saved by the death of Jesus on the cross. Once again, the Orthodox liturgical tradition reads back into an earlier event in the life of Jesus the consequences of Good Friday and Easter. But there is in the New Testament a connection between Jesus' baptism and the cross. In St Luke's Gospel Jesus says, 'I have a baptism with which to be baptized, and what stress I am under until it is completed!' (Luke 12.50). He is referring to his death, which he describes as a baptism. Already in his baptism in the Jordan he had dedicated himself to a life of doing his Father's will. That acceptance of his vocation then would lead inexorably to the baptism of the cross.

The baptism of Jesus is the pattern for Christian baptism. When we are washed at the font, we receive the Holy Spirit, and we are proclaimed to be sons and daughters of the Father, sisters and brothers of Jesus Christ with whom we have been

clothed. Our baptism, like his, commits us to live in accordance with his and our Father's will. That will is that we
should love him and love our neighbour as ourselves. Doing
that means dying to our fallen selves, and letting the Holy
Spirit raise us to share the new life of the crucified and risen
Christ, within the love of God the Holy Trinity. That love
was revealed at Jesus' baptism in Jordan, and in the waters of
death that overwhelmed him on the cross. From those waters
was born the new and eternal life we can enjoy now as the
free gift of God.

Synaxis of St John the Baptist
7 January

John the Baptist, a cousin of Jesus, led a prophetic movement
among the Jews, a little before Jesus began his own ministry.
He called people to repent in view of the imminent coming of
the kingdom of God, and practised baptism as a sign of
repentance. Derived most probably from Jewish proselyte
baptism, it was remarkable for being applied to Jews themselves. It seem that for a while John and his disciples worked
independently of Jesus and his disciples, perhaps to some
extent in competition. After John's execution by Herod, Jesus
continued to proclaim the coming kingdom, and in time John
came to be seen by the Christian community as preparing the
way for Jesus, and so subordinate to him. This development
can be traced within the Gospels, which portray John as
Elijah, wearing a garment made of hair and a leather belt (cf. 2
Kings 1.8), and fulfilling the prophecy in Malachi 4.5–6.
There God promises to send Elijah the prophet before the
'great and terrible day of the Lord'. Christian faith saw in
Jesus God's promised Messiah, and in John God's messenger
Elijah.

So in Christian tradition John the Baptist is celebrated as
the Precursor of Jesus Christ, the one who prepared his way.
The Orthodox Church commemorates him appropriately the

77

day after the Theophany, the manifestation of Jesus as the Son of God at his baptism, John's chief work. That continues to be the main theme of the texts for today, which celebrate John as the baptizer of Jesus.

The icon of John the Baptist depicts him in the desert, wearing a garment of hair, holding a cross, and with a scroll in which are written the words, 'Repent, for the kingdom of heaven is at hand'. His severed head is often shown separately on a dish, on the ground, at the feet of the living John, as an indication of the way he met his death. Sometimes John is shown with wings, like an angel. This is because Luke 7.27 identifies John as the promised messenger of Malachi 3.1, sent to prepare the way of Christ. In Greek the word for messenger is *angelos*, translated as 'angel' when the messenger is from God.

FROM VESPERS

Illustrious Precursor of Christ,
Baptist inspired by God,
reverently we bless you
and glorify Christ,
who bowed his head to you
in the Jordan,
and made holy
mortal human nature.
Pray him then to give us peace
and abundant mercy.

Looking down,
wise Precursor John,
you saw the Father's glory,
which cannot be told,
the Son in the water;
and the Spirit descending
like a dove,

purifying and illuminating
earth's farthest bounds.
So we praise you,
who serve the mysteries
of the Trinity,
and honour your holy festival.

Embodied lamp,
Saviour's Precursor,
offspring of barren woman,
friend of Virgin's Son,
whom you worshipped,
leaping in the womb,
whom you baptized
in Jordan's waters:
we ask you, prophet,
to pray to him,
that we may escape
the coming storm.

When he saw you, Lord,
coming to him,
John the Precursor was astonished,
and like a prudent slave
he cried out in fear:
What kind of humility is this,
Saviour?
What kind of poverty is this,
with which you have clothed yourself?
Rich in goodness,
you have put on
our humbled humanity,
and in your compassion
have raised us up.

Come to me today,
as I accomplish a mystery,
said the Saviour of all
in reply to the Precursor,
serve me with awe,
and do not be afraid.
For I am baptized as a man
in Jordan's waters,
in which you see me,
though by nature I am unstained,
and so I renew Adam,
destroyed by sin.

The memory of the righteous is praised;
but for you, his Precursor,
the Lord's witness suffices.
For you have been shown
to be truly more honoured
than the prophets,
for you have been deemed fit
to baptize in the waters
him whom they foretold.
Having then contended
for the truth,
you had the joy
of proclaiming to those in Hell
God revealed in flesh,
who takes away the world's sin,
and gives us abundant mercy.

FROM MATINS

Jordan was afraid
when you came in bodily form,
and turned back in terror.
John stepped back in fear,

as he carried out
his spiritual ministry.
The angelic hosts were terrified
when they saw you in the waters,
being baptized in the body.
All who sat in darkness
were enlightened,
and praised you,
for you have revealed yourself,
and filled all things with light.

To Adam, who lost his sight in Eden,
the Sun appeared in Bethlehem,
and opened his eyes,
washing them in Jordan's waters.
The light which never sets
has dawned on him
whom black night shrouded
with thick darkness.
No longer is it night for him,
but always day.
Day's first light
has dawned for him,
for in the cool of the day
he hid himself,
as it is written.
He has found the light,
which has raised him up.
He who fell towards evening
has been set free from darkness,
and has attained the dawn
which has been revealed,
and illuminates all things.

From barren womb you emerged,
Baptist, an angelic messenger;

from earliest childhood
you lived in the desert;
you showed yourself seal
of all the prophets.
For you were deemed fit
to baptize in the Jordan
the one whom they saw in many forms
and spoke of in words hard to understand.
You heard the Father's voice from heaven,
which testified to his Sonship.
You saw the Spirit in the form of a dove,
drawing down the voice on the one baptized.
You are above all the prophets:
pray always for us
who commemorate you in faith.

Like that of his greater cousin, Jesus, John's birth was the result of divine intervention, for John has his part to play in the drama of salvation. St Luke's Gospel tells the story of his annunciation and birth, in parallel to those of Jesus. That story portrays John as aware from his conception of the greatness of Jesus. When Mary went to visit her cousin Elizabeth, John leaped for joy in his mother's womb (Luke 1.39–45). It was the beginning of his witness to Jesus as the Messiah, whose way he had been born to prepare. Matthew, Mark and Luke all associate John with Isaiah's prophecy of the Lord's coming and the preparation of his way (Isaiah 40.3–5). John goes before Jesus, and so has the title in Orthodox tradition of Precursor, or Forerunner. He is the greatest of the prophets, announcing the fulfilment of their predictions of the coming Saviour; and John's witness to Jesus as the Christ is a recurring theme of today's hymns.

In Orthodox tradition John the Baptist is known as 'the friend of the bridegroom', from John's answer to his disciples in St John's Gospel (3.27–30). This is the passage in which John is most clearly subordinated to Jesus, and concludes with

John's affirmation, 'He must increase, but I must decrease'. After Mary, he is the most powerful intercessor for human-kind. In the iconographic composition known as the Deesis, or intercession, Jesus is depicted enthroned, with Mary and John the Baptist on either side, inclined towards Jesus in supplication. The liturgical texts frequently ask John to pray for us.

Christian tradition associates the Church with Christ himself: it is his body, his bride. But there is also a sense in which the Church can rightly be associated with John the Baptist. For the Church is called to witness to Jesus as the Messiah, and to point the world to him, as the one in whom God's purpose for his creation is fulfilled. John is depicted, too, particularly by St Luke, as within the great prophetic tradition of Israel in calling for social justice (Luke 3.7–14). This aspect of John's ministry does not feature prominently in the Orthodox hymns for the feast. Yet in this too the Church is called to follow John, by calling and working for God's compassion and justice in all human relationships.

6 PRESENTATION OF CHRIST

When Jesus was forty days old Mary and Joseph brought him to the temple in Jerusalem 'to present him to the Lord' (Luke 2.22), in accordance with the regulations laid down in Leviticus 12. St Luke is the only evangelist to include this episode (Luke 2.22–38), and he depicts a scene of ideal Old Testament piety, in harmony with the rest of his infancy narrative. Written up in the light of subsequent Christian faith in the crucified and risen Jesus as the Son of God, the account presents Jesus as the awaited 'light for revelation to the Gentiles' (Isaiah 42.6 and 49.6). He is the Messiah who brings the light of God's salvation to all peoples, both Jews and Gentiles.

Simeon and Anna stand for all that is best in the religion of Israel. Simeon is 'righteous and devout, looking forward to the consolation of Israel'; Anna is a prophet who 'never left the temple but worshipped there with fasting and prayer day and night'. In welcoming Jesus they welcome the fulfilment of Israel's hopes, and so, in Luke's narrative, symbolize the transition from the first covenant to the new, to whose beginning they bear witness. Their commemoration follows naturally after the feast of the Presentation, or Meeting of Christ, as the Orthodox call it. Similar themes run through the texts for their commemoration as for the feast itself.

St Luke's story provides the basic material for the hymns for the feast; and here, as in preceding feasts, the narrative is interpreted in the light of the fully developed understanding of the person of Jesus worked out by the ecumenical councils.

The icon of the feast depicts the scene as Luke describes it. Against a background of a representation of the temple, Mary and Joseph advance with the child, Joseph carrying two doves. Simeon, his hands covered with a cloth to receive with due honour the Christ-child, inclines towards him, while

Christ blesses Simeon. Anna is close by, and sometimes holds a scroll with the words, 'This child has created heaven and earth'.

Forefeast of the Meeting of Our Lord Jesus Christ
1 February

FROM VESPERS

The illustrious temple
prepares to welcome the Lord,
who comes as a child,
and enlightens
with spiritual gifts
its faithful and devout assembly.
To him it calls out:
You, Word of God,
are the glory and praise
and adornment of my people,
and for my sake
you have become incarnate,
a child.

Most holy Simeon,
come and see, in the temple,
Christ, the hope
which you hold.
Take him in your arms
and cry out:
Now, Saviour, release me
your servant from this earth.
Call the prophetess Anna,
that with you
she may glorify the Benefactor,

who has been born a child,
in awesome way, incarnate.

The light which shines
thrice-brighter than the sun,
shines clearly from the Virgin
in a way that is new:
with the brilliant light
of resplendent divinity,
it has enlightened all things
beyond power of telling.

The heavenly vaults'
celestial choir
stoops earthward down,
and sees him brought,
a sucking child,
firstborn of all creation,
into the temple,
carried by mother
who knows not man.
In song now with us, awestruck,
they anticipate the feast.

FROM MATINS

You were born on earth,
who are with the Father
without beginning.
You have been brought
into the temple,
whom nothing can contain.
With joy old Simeon
took you in his hands
and cried out:
Now release me,

whom you have sought out,
in accordance with your word;
for you have freely willed
as God to save the human race.

The ages' treasure
and the life of all,
you became a child for me,
born under the Law,
who once on Mount Sinai
on tablets inscribed the Law.
You came to release everyone
from the Law's former slavery.
Glory to your compassion, Saviour;
glory to your kingdom;
glory to your saving purpose!
You alone love humankind.

You who believe,
today open your hearts,
as though they were arms;
and with purified minds
welcome the Lord who comes,
celebrating the feast
with song in advance.

The most pure Maiden
brought the child
into the temple,
and so fulfilled the Law.
As righteous Simeon
took him in his arms,
he said to the Virgin:
This child is destined
for the falling and rising

of many, and to be a sign
in the world.

Meeting of Our Lord Jesus Christ
2 February

FROM VESPERS

Come, go we too
with songs inspired
to meet Christ,
and welcome him
whose salvation Simeon saw.
This is he
whom David foretold:
this is he
who spoke through the prophets,
who was incarnate for us,
and speaks by the Law.
Him let us worship.

Let heaven's gate today be opened;
for the Father's Word,
who knows no beginning,
in time begins to be,
yet does not abandon
his divine nature.
By Virgin Mother is he brought,
a forty-days-old child,
willingly to the Law's temple.
The old man takes him in his arms:
Release me, cries
the servant to the Master,
for my eyes have seen your salvation.
You have come into the world

to save the human race:
glory to you!

Today old Simeon,
in spirit rejoicing,
comes into the temple,
to take in his arms
him who gave the Law to Moses
and is the Law's fulfilment.
Moses was deemed fit
to see God in darkness
and by hidden voice;
his face veiled,
he rebuked the Hebrews'
faithless hearts.
Simeon held the Father's Word,
eternally begotten,
become incarnate,
and revealed the nations' light,
the cross and resurrection.
Anna was revealed
as a prophetess,
proclaiming the Saviour
and Israel's deliverer.
To him let us cry: Christ our God,
at the prayers of the Mother of God,
have mercy on us.

FROM MATINS

The Ancient of Days
becomes for me a child;
the most pure God
accepts purification,
to confirm the reality
of the humanity

he took of the Virgin.
Initiated into these mysteries,
Simeon recognized him as God
appearing in flesh.
As Life he greeted him,
and with gladness
cried out in old age:
Release me;
for I have seen you,
the Life of all.

Of old on Mount Sinai
Moses saw God's back,
and was deemed fit,
in darkness and tempest,
dimly to hear God's voice.
Now Simeon has taken
in his arms God,
for us incarnate,
yet unchanged;
with joy has he sped
from here below
to life eternal.
So he cried out:
Now, Master,
let your servant go.

When he came to the temple,
guided by the Spirit,
the old man took in his arms
the Law's master and cried out:
Now from the fetters of the flesh
release me in peace
as you promised.
For with my own eyes I have seen

your revelation to the nations
and Israel's salvation.

As a light
for revelation to the nations
have you appeared, Lord,
seated on a swift cloud
as the Sun of righteousness;
you have fulfilled
the Law's shadows,
displayed new grace's
first beginnings.
So when he saw you,
Simeon called out:
From corruption release me,
for today I have seen you.

Commemoration of Sts Simeon and Anna

3 February

FROM VESPERS

Simeon took in his arms,
from the Virgin's hands,
the Saviour begotten
before time began,
and he cried out:
The ends of the earth
have seen the light
of your glory.
Now release your servant,
good Master, in peace,
for I have seen you.

Young in spirit,
but in body old,

you were told, Simeon,
you would not see death
before you had seen
the young child,
the eternal Creator,
the God of all,
who became poor
by taking flesh.
When you saw him
you leaped in joy
and asked release
from the body.
So you passed, rejoicing,
to the divine dwellings.

God-inspired Anna
and most happy Simeon,
blameless before the Law,
radiant with prophecy,
saw the Law's giver,
revealed for us a child,
and worshipped him.
Today we keep
with joy their feast,
in duty bound,
giving glory to Jesus,
who loves humankind.

The Ancient of Days,
become child incarnate,
is brought to the temple
by the Virgin his Mother,
fulfilling the promise
his own Law had made.
Simeon received him and said:
Now let your servant depart in peace,

according to your word;
for my eyes have seen,
holy Lord, your salvation.

FROM MATINS

He who is full
has emptied himself,
he who eternally is
begins to be,
the Word becomes flesh,
the Creator is formed,
the Infinite is embraced,
becoming incarnate,
in your womb,
you who are favoured by God.

Holy Simeon, rejoicing,
took you in his arms, O Christ,
incarnate of the Virgin.
He cried out:
Now you let your servant go, Master.
Blameless Anna, too,
prophetess and glorified,
bore you witness
and gave you praise.
We cry out to you, Life-giver:
Glory to you,
who has willed it so!

Grown old in years,
in faith grown young,
Simeon desired to see
the child young and perfect,
who makes new
a world grown old

under the onslaught
of its ancient foe.

Wise prophetess Anna
and old renowned Simeon,
like sun and moon,
shed beams of spiritual light
on all that moves beneath the sun.
For their sake deliver us,
Lord and lover of humankind,
from the darkness of our sins.

When he saw you coming,
God's Mother and Birthgiver,
the old man spoke
as a prophet:
See, your son is destined
for the falling and rising
of many, Lady,
and for a sign
hard to interpret.

The Meeting commemorates an event in the life of Jesus
Christ. But as always, the liturgical celebration involves us as
well. As the hymns make clear, we are invited to go and meet
Christ, who comes to us, and welcome him.

Mary and Joseph brought Jesus to the temple in Jerusalem,
where he met representatives of his people. The temple was
the place which God had chosen under the first covenant,
where his presence could be found, and worship to him
offered. Jesus was critical of the temple: he once drove out
those who bought and sold, in a prophetic act which perhaps
looked towards the replacement of the old temple by a new,
in the new age of God's kingdom (cf. Mark 11.15–19). That
new temple, the New Testament affirms, is none other than
Jesus himself. St John, in his account of that event, has Jesus

say that if the temple were to be destroyed, he would raise it up in three days; and when the people were incredulous, John comments: 'But he spoke of the temple of his body' (John 2.13–22).

The new temple of God which is the body of Jesus is a growing body. St Paul insists that all who come to faith in Jesus and are baptized, are baptized into Christ and become members of his body. That means they become living stones in the temple of God which is the body of Christ, and themselves individually temples of the Holy Spirit (1 Corinthians 3.16). So through the Spirit Christ lives in us, and we are to offer him, in the temple of our own selves, the spiritual worship of lives dedicated to him (Romans 12.1).

But that is only one aspect of the truth. For it is also the case that we have to become the living temples that we already in principle are, and let Christ who comes to us in the Holy Spirit dwell in us more fully. The Christian life, according to the conversation of Nicholas Motovilov with St Seraphim of Sarov, consists in acquiring the Holy Spirit. That is another way of saying that the life of Christ has to grow in us. Christ in the Spirit is constantly coming to meet us, in the circumstances of daily life, and in other people, particularly those in any kind of need. He comes to us who are his temple, in order that that we may receive him into our lives more fully, and so become still more his temple.

Simeon and Anna welcomed the Messiah promised to the People of God under the first covenant. Themselves within the prophetic tradition, they recognized the one whom the prophets had foretold. Since then, Christians have believed that the Messiah has come: we have seen God's salvation in Jesus Christ. Yet we recognize too that the fulfilment of his saving work is for the future, even if its first-fruits are with us now. Messiah has come in humility, but he will come in glory. So we can see in Simeon and Anna types of ourselves. Like them, we are to be ready and waiting for Christ to come. Like them, we have already received the gift of the Spirit, enabling us to perceive him when he does come. We are to welcome him into the temple of ourselves, who are living stones in the temple of the Christian community. So we set ourselves, through prayer, worship, and our endeavour to live according to the commandments of love, to become increasingly sensitive to his coming; and as we grow in our ability to receive him, his life in us is strengthened, and God's salvation is seen more clearly.

7 ANNUNCIATION

It is Luke who includes in his infancy narrative the story of the annunciation to Mary of the birth of Jesus. Like his story of the announcement of John the Baptist's birth, it resembles in some respects the Old Testament stories of the miraculous conceptions of such great figures in Israel's history as Samson (Judges 13) and Samuel (1 Samuel 1). The Magnificat, Mary's hymn of praise to God in Luke's Gospel, is closely modelled on the Song of Hannah (1 Samuel 2).

The Gospel according to Mark, usually held to be the earliest of the four Gospels, begins with the first public appearance of Jesus and his baptism. The stories of his birth, with which Matthew and Luke preface their Gospels, reflect Christian faith after the resurrection in Jesus 'who was descended from David according to the flesh and was declared to be Son of God with power according to the Spirit of holiness by resurrection from the dead' (Romans 1.3–4). That faith in Jesus as the Son of God was expressed in the fourth century by the phrase in the Nicene Creed 'conceived by the Holy Spirit, born of the Virgin Mary'. Luke's account is evidence for early belief in the virginal conception of Jesus, and affirms his birth to be due entirely to the action of God.

The themes of the texts for the Annunciation come from Luke's account. They are drawn too from the early comparison and contrast of Mary with Eve: Eve who disobeys and so brings about the Fall and the loss of paradise, Mary whose willing acceptance of God's will reverses her ancestor's disobedience. This contrast is parallel to that found earlier in Paul's letters between the first Adam, the pattern of fallen humanity, and Jesus Christ, the new Adam, the model and source of humanity renewed and reconciled with God.

Throughout, the texts reflect the dogmatic definitions of the first four ecumenical councils regarding the divinity of

Jesus Christ and his relation to the Father: it is the divine Word, the Second Person of the Trinity, who enters Mary's womb and there takes our human nature upon himself. They reflect too the emphasis on the purity of Mary, understood in terms of virginity, which we have seen first attested in the *Protevangelium of James* in the second century. The belief that Mary's virginity was preserved not only before, but also after, the birth of Jesus became an integral part of the Church's tradition concerning Mary from the fourth century onwards.

The icon of the feast is based chiefly on Luke's narrative. But sometimes it includes details taken from the *Protevangelium of James*, which elaborates Luke's story. Mary is said to have been drawing out purple thread for a veil for the temple when Gabriel came to her; and this detail is occasionally included in the scene. The icon depicts Gabriel coming to Mary to tell her of the child she will conceive. By contrast with Western pictures of the Annunciation, where Mary is often shown kneeling in prayer, in the icon she is depicted sometimes seated, at others standing. The Holy Spirit is often shown coming towards her in the form of a dove, within a ray of light from heaven.

Forefeast of the Annunciation of the Mother of God

24 March

FROM VESPERS

The hidden mystery,
unknown to angels,
is entrusted to the archangel Gabriel.
Now he will come to you,
fair undefiled turtledove,
humankind's revival;
he will cry out,

holy Lady, to you:
Greetings! prepare to receive
by my word in your womb
God the Word.

A palace filled with light,
the divine maiden's undefiled womb
is prepared for you, Lord:
In it come down and dwell,
having mercy on your creation;
under attack through envy,
in bondage to the Evil One,
its primal beauty lost,
it waits for you
to descend and save it.

The archangel Gabriel,
in visible form,
will come to you, Pure One,
and cry out to you:
Hail, curse's redemption,
you raise up the fallen!
Hail, you alone chosen,
who gave answer to God!
Hail, Sun's living cloud!
Receive him who though bodiless
yet wills to dwell in your womb.

Today the beginning
of the whole world's joy
prompts us to praise
its forefeast.
For see, Gabriel comes,
bringing good news
to the Virgin,
and cries out to her:

Greetings, favoured one,
the Lord is with you!

FROM MATINS

Today all creation rejoices,
for the angel cries: Greetings!
Blessed are you, Pure One,
Christ's spotless Mother.
Today is the serpent's
haughtiness bridled,
for the bonds
of our ancestor's curse are undone.
We too then cry out to you:
Greetings, most favoured one!

Without ceasing to sit
on the Father's right,
he who is beyond all being
will make his dwelling,
pure Lady, in you;
so that he might set you,
who are close to him and good,
on his right like a Queen,
and stretch out his right hand
to all the fallen, and save us.

As gifts before the festival
we bring you, purest Lady,
the wealth of our poverty:
purity and self-control,
praise, prayers and tears,
fasting and meekness.
For their sake, Lady,
help and protect us all,
Mother of God, in your mercy.

God's Birthgiver heard
speech she knew not.
For the archangel announced
to her the good news.
Accepting in faith the greeting,
she conceived you,
who are God from all eternity.
So we too rejoice
and cry out to you:
O God, become flesh
through her, without change,
grant peace to the world
and great mercy to us.

Annunciation of the Mother of God
25 March

FROM VESPERS

The Creator, pitying his creation
and stooping in his compassion,
makes haste to dwell in a Maiden's womb,
the womb of God's own child.
The great archangel came to her
and said: Greetings,
whom God has favoured!
Our God is now with you.
Have no fear of me,
the king's great commander.
For you have found the grace
which your ancestress Eve
lost of old.
You will conceive
and give birth to him

who is of one being
with the Father.

From heaven was sent
the archangel Gabriel,
to announce to the Virgin
her conceiving.
He came to Nazareth
and, considering the wonder
in his mind, was amazed:
How can he be born of a Virgin
who, beyond understanding, dwells on high?
How can he, whose throne is heaven
and whose footstool earth,
be embraced in a woman's womb?
He on whom the six-winged seraphs
and cherubim with many eyes
cannot intently look,
has consented at a single word
to become flesh through her.
He who is present is the Word of God.
So why do I stand still
and not say to the maiden:
Greetings, favoured one!
the Lord is with you.
Greetings, pure Virgin!
Greetings, unmarried Bride!
Greetings, Life's mother!
Blessed is the fruit of your womb!

Today is our salvation's beginning,
the eternal mystery's revealing.
God's Son
becomes the Virgin's;
Gabriel
brings good news of grace.

Join we then him
and sing to God's Mother:
Greetings, favoured one!
The Lord is with you.

FROM GREAT COMPLINE

In the sixth month
the archangel Gabriel
was sent from heaven
to a town in Galilee,
called Nazareth,
to bring to the Virgin
the joyful good news.
He came to her and said:
Greetings, favoured one!
The Lord is with you.
Greetings, vessel holding
the nature nothing can contain!
For your womb, blessed one,
has embraced him
whom the heavens could not contain.
Greetings, honoured Lady!
You are Adam's renewal
and Eve's liberation,
the whole world's rejoicing,
our race's great joy.

Heavens, be merry
and earth, rejoice!
for he who with the Father
is co-eternal,
without beginning,
and shares his throne,
has displayed his compassion
and loving mercy for humankind.

In accordance with the Father's
loving will and wise counsel,
he has stooped to empty himself,
and taken up his abode
in a virgin womb,
purified for him by the Spirit.
O what marvel!
God is with us;
a womb embraces the infinite;
the timeless is within time.
Marvellous is his conception,
without seed!
Beyond telling
his self-emptying!
How great the mystery!
For God empties himself,
becomes incarnate,
becomes a creature,
and to a Virgin
the angel announces
her conceiving:
Greetings, favoured one!
The Lord is with you,
in his abundant mercy.

Today is joy's good news,
the Virgin's festival.
Earth's joined with heaven,
Adam's made anew,
from earliest sadness
is Eve set free.
For our nature's tent,
made Godlike by him
who took upon himself
our human clay,
is made God's own temple.

O mystery!
How he empties himself
cannot be known;
how he is conceived
cannot be told.
The angel officiates at the marvel;
the Virgin's womb accepts the Son;
the Holy Spirit is sent from above;
the Father consents from heaven,
common purpose brings about the covenant.
In him and by him we are saved:
cry we out then with Gabriel
to the Virgin:
Greetings, favoured one!
The Lord is with you.
From her our salvation,
Christ our God,
has taken our human nature,
exalting it to himself.
Pray to him to save us.

FROM MATINS

Gabriel from heaven
called to the holy one:
Greetings! for you will conceive
in your womb the God
who is before all ages,
who by his word
established earth's bounds.
To which Mary replied:
Husbandless am I:
how shall I bear a son?
Who has seen
seedless birth?
The angel explained

to the Virgin, God's Mother:
The Holy Spirit
will come upon you,
and the power of the Most High
will overshadow you.

God's Word to earth
has now come down.
Standing before the Virgin
the angel cried:
Greetings, blessed one!
You alone have kept
virginity's seal,
when you received in your womb
the Word and Lord
who is before all ages,
that as God he might save
from error our human race.

From the Father eternally,
from his Mother in time
the Word above all being
is revealed to the world.
He takes the form of a slave
and becomes human,
not parted from God.
He creates Adam anew
in the womb of her
who without seed conceived him.

The Annunciation is first and most obviously the announcement of the conception and birth of Jesus. The texts emphasize that it is God who is to be born of the Virgin as a human
being, one of his own creatures. By being united with its
Creator, humanity is created anew in the divine image and
likeness.

But Mary, although she is the mother of Jesus the Christ, is also in Christian tradition the figure of the Church, the People of God. In the Orthodox Church she is never separated from the Church she signifies. Her vocation is therefore also the vocation of the Church, which is called to bring Christ into the world. As we have seen, this is visually demonstrated in the iconography of an Orthodox church, where in the semidome of the apse there is usually to be found an image of the Mother of God. The immediate reference is to the Eucharist, celebrated at the altar in the sanctuary below. As Mary, by the power of the Holy Spirit, brought forth Christ, so the Church, in celebrating the Eucharist, brings him into the world, invoking the Holy Spirit to make the eucharistic gifts the body and blood of Christ, the sacramental signs of his presence.

Mary's vocation belongs to every Christian, as well as to the Christian community as a whole. Through our willing obedience to the word of God, the Holy Spirit dwells within us, in the depths of our being, and there forms Christ in us. We bring him forth in our world, as we learn to let his mind inform ours, and as we put into practice the love of God, which was embodied in him, and shed abroad in human hearts by the Holy Spirit. The Annunciation reminds us that we too are overshadowed by the power of the Most High, that Christ is to be formed in us, and that we are to be the means by whom the love of God enters the world, to extend in its life his reconciling and renewing power.

Synaxis of the Archangel Gabriel
26 March

Gabriel is commemorated with Michael, the chief of the angels, and all the 'bodiless powers of heaven' on 8 November. But as the messenger of God who played an essential part in the story of the annunciation he is properly commemorated by himself today. The texts for the day emphasize particularly his role in the annunciation to Mary, though they also mention the annunciation to Zechariah. Some are requests for his prayers and protection.

Angels are spiritual beings, and so normally invisible. But they have appeared in visible form, and so can be depicted on icons, in human form but with wings. Gabriel forms part of the icon of the annunciation, and is also depicted by himself, and with Michael. He may be shown as a warrior, or as a peaceful messenger, in either case full-length or in bust form. He is always beardless, like all the angels, with long, curly hair and androgynous features. Sometimes he, like Michael, is shown holding a sphere in one hand, with the sign of Christ on it.

FROM VESPERS

Gabriel most mighty,
understanding most godlike,
radiant and heavenly,
who with the hosts above
looks upon the Light
bright as three suns,
came and announced
to the Virgin
the good news of the mystery
awesome and divine;
he prays for us.

The great mystery,
unknown before to the angels
and hidden from all ages,
was entrusted
to you, Gabriel, alone;
when you came to Nazareth
you were bold
to tell it to her

who alone is pure.
With her, pray there be given us
peace and great mercy.

Excellent Gabriel,
angels' commander,
filled ever with light,
you obey the commands
and accomplish the will
of the Almighty;
protect those
who honour you,
giving you love,
and pray always
there be given us
peace and great mercy.

Great captain
of the heavenly hosts,
we ask you, though unworthy,
by your prayers to protect us
with the covering wings
of your spiritual glory;
and guard us who bow
before you and cry:
Deliver us from all need,
for you are commander
of the powers on high.

FROM MATINS

To you, Gabriel, the chief
of God's spiritual servants,
was entrusted the mystery,
awe-inspiring indeed,
ordained before the ages:

the holy Virgin's
childbirth beyond telling.
You cried out to her:
Greetings, favoured one!
So we who believe,
as we ought, joyfully
bless you at all times.

Illumined by participation
in the original Mind,
you appeared a second light,
crying out with the
countless angelic hosts:
Holy is God,
the Maker of all;
holy the Son,
like him without beginning;
holy the Spirit,
with them enthroned.

Commander of the angels,
you are the glorious servant
of the radiant Trinity,
awesome, revered
and Creator of all.
So pray for us now,
mediator unceasing,
that we may be saved
from all need and pain.
So we may cry out to you:
Greetings, your servants' protector!

Of John's birth, glorious angel,
you once told Zechariah,
as he stood in God's temple,
praising God the Redeemer:

Blessed are you,
God and Lord of our fathers,
praised above all.

You stand before the throne of God,
who shines with threefold light;
you are yourself illumined
with the divine radiance,
ever streaming thence.
Free from passions' darkness
those who on earth
rejoice and praise you;
protect them with your light,
Gabriel, great commander,
who pray always for us.

Christianity inherited belief in angels from Israelite religion. In the Old Testament angels form a heavenly court in the presence of God, whom they worship and praise, and whose will they do in the life of nations and individuals. The word 'angel' in Greek means messenger, and one of their functions is to communicate with human beings. Gabriel is found in the Book of Daniel, giving him information about the future, and Michael is named there, too, as the protector of Israel. In the New Testament angels attend Jesus at critical moments in his ministry, worship God in heaven, and will accompany Jesus at his return. It is Gabriel who gives to Mary the good news of the conception of Jesus.

Veneration of the angels was particularly strong in the East, where Christian belief in angels was systematized by Pseudo-Dionysius the Areopagite in the early sixth century. He arranged the angelic hosts in three hierarchies, each made up of three choirs. In the first were seraphim, cherubim and thrones; in the second, dominations, virtues and powers; and in the third, principalities, archangels and angels. It is only the last two which have dealings with humankind.

Gabriel, 'the light of God', came to be identified in Christian tradition with the angel who announced the births of Samson, John the Baptist, and the Mother of God. It was he who fed Mary in the temple, who told the shepherds of the birth of Christ, and who spoke to Joseph in his dreams. With Michael, who is warrior rather than messenger, Gabriel leads the angelic hosts; and with all the angels and archangels he prays for God's people. The two angelic chiefs often appear in the Deesis, the iconographic composition which depicts various saints interceding with Christ for humankind.

The texts for today speak of the mystery of the incarnation, entrusted to Gabriel, and of the part he played in the annunciation. They dwell too on the radiance of the archangel, who shines with the brightness of the divine light in which he stands. By that light he protects those who invoke his prayers.

8 Transfiguration

The transfiguration of Jesus, described in the Gospels according to Matthew (17.1–9), Mark (9.2–10) and Luke (9.28–36), is one of the most mysterious of the events recounted in the life of Jesus. Taking Peter, James and John, Jesus goes up a high mountain, which tradition identifies as Mount Tabor in Galilee. There he is transfigured, his face shines like the sun, and his clothes become white as light. Moses and Elijah appear, talking with him. They demonstrate the witness of the Law and the Prophets of Israel to Jesus as Messiah. The voice from heaven, which has already proclaimed Jesus' divine Sonship at his baptism, does so again here. In all three Gospels the story ends with Jesus' command to the three disciples, to tell no one about the vision until the Son of Man is raised from the dead. The themes of the texts are taken from the gospel story, interpreted in the light of theological reflection on the meaning of the event.

The icon of the feast depicts the gospel story. In the centre on a mountain peak Jesus is shown within a mandorla, an almond-shaped panel symbolizing the glory of divinity. His clothing gleams, and from him come rays of light, often painted in the gold which is another symbol of divinity. They fall on the three disciples, who are prostrate on the ground below him. They fall too on the landscape all round. On either side of Jesus are Moses and Elijah, each standing on his own peak.

Forefeast of the Transfiguration of Our Lord Jesus Christ

5 August

FROM VESPERS

Come, let us go up with Jesus,
who climbs the holy mount,
and there let us listen
to the voice of the living God,
of the Father without beginning,
which through the bright cloud
bore witness in the divine Spirit
to the reality of the eternal Sonship;
and, enlightened in our minds,
let us in light see Light.

Come now, being transformed
with a better transformation,
let us prepare ourselves well
for tomorrow's festival;
let us ascend God's holy mountain,
to see Christ's unchanged glory,
shining brighter than the sun.
Enlightened with threefold light,
by it let us praise his humility.

Come, let us go up
to the mountain of the Lord,
and to the house of our God,
and let us see the glory
of his transfiguration,
glory as of the Father's only Son.
In light let us receive Light,
and, exalted by the Spirit,

let us praise the Trinity,
one in Being, for ever.

Christ our God, on Mount Tabor
you were transfigured in glory,
and you displayed to the disciples
the glory of your divinity:
enlighten us with the light
of your knowledge,
and guide us in the way
of your commandments;
for you are good
and you love humankind.

FROM MATINS

Today we who believe keep
with splendour the forefeast
of the glorious and awesome
transfiguration of Christ;
and with one voice we cry out:
Transform, O Saviour,
the confusion of our nature,
enlighten it with your divine body,
and in your mercy restore to it
the incorruption it once enjoyed.
For we all praise you,
our only God.

By the divine transfiguration
of our human form,
once defaced by wickedness,
the Creator today has saved
our forefather Adam from corruption,
from the hidden depths of Hades,
and has made our mind divine;

God and humanity have come together,
the two natures united
without confusion or change,
without division or separation.
So he has shone forth on Tabor
in manner beyond telling,
and from his whole body
he has shed forth
the rays of his divinity,
illuminating those who cry out:
Let Christ be transfigured,
and so save us all.

We who desire only
the divine glory,
let us pierce the cloud
of our earthly body,
and ascend Mount Tabor.
Let us make every effort
to be deemed fit,
with Moses and Elijah,
with the chosen disciples,
to be partakers
of divine radiance
which none can approach,
by light receiving Light.

Come, let us ascend the holy mountain,
and by faith see the Lord's
resplendent transfiguration.
In faith let us worship him, saying:
You alone are our God,
who became human
and made human nature divine.

Moses, who saw God,
and Elijah, who went up
unburnt in a chariot of fire
on his way to heaven,
saw you in the cloud,
who gave and fulfilled
the Law and the prophets,
and bore witness to you
at your transfiguration.
Lord, make us fit with them,
to share in your light,
that we may praise you for ever.

Transfiguration of Our Lord Jesus Christ

6 August

FROM VESPERS

Before your crucifixion, Lord,
you took the disciples up a high mountain,
and were transfigured in their presence,
shedding upon them the light of your power.
Both from love of humankind,
and to display your authority,
you wished to show them
the radiance of the resurrection.
Make us too, O God,
fit to see it in peace,
for you are merciful,
and you love humankind.

When you prefigured your resurrection,
Christ our God,
you took your three disciples,
Peter and James and John,

and went to the top of Mount Tabor;
And when, Saviour, you were transfigured,
Mount Tabor was overspread with light.
Your disciples, Word of God,
threw themselves down on the ground,
for they could not bear to look
at the form which cannot be seen.
The angels in attendance
were afraid and trembled,
the heavens shuddered,
the earth quaked,
when they saw on earth
the Lord of glory.

On Mount Tabor, Christ our God,
you were transfigured in glory,
and you showed the disciples
your divinity's glory:
shed upon us too
the light of your knowledge,
and lead us in the ways of your laws,
you who alone are good,
and love humankind.

He who once spoke with Moses
in symbols on Mount Sinai,
and said: I am he who is,
today, transfigured on Mount Tabor
in the presence of the disciples,
displayed the beautiful archetype of the image,
in himself exalting human nature.
Of this great grace he made
Moses and Elijah witnesses;
and so made partakers of joy
those who announced in advance

the exodus accomplished by the cross
and saving resurrection.

When he foresaw in spirit
your only-begotten Son's
coming among us in the flesh,
God's ancestor, David, from afar
summoned creation to make merry.
He prophesied and cried out:
Tabor and Hermon
will rejoice in your name.
For when you had gone up the mountain,
Saviour, with your disciples,
you were transfigured,
and made human nature,
darkened in Adam,
once again shine forth,
changing it into the glory and radiance
of your own divine nature.
So we cry out to you:
Glory to you, Lord,
Creator of all.

To Peter and John and James,
your chosen disciples,
you showed today, Lord,
on Mount Tabor the glory
of your divine form.
For they saw your clothing
shine as the light,
and your face
more radiant than the sun.
They could not endure the sight
of your unbearable brightness,
and fell down on the ground,
quite unable to look up.

For they heard a voice,
bearing witness from above:
This is my beloved Son,
who has come into the world
to save humankind.

FROM MATINS

When you were transfigured, Saviour,
on Mount Tabor, you showed gloriously
the transformation human beings will undergo
at your second and awesome coming.
Elijah and Moses spoke with you,
and you called the three disciples
to be with you.
When they saw your glory, Lord,
they were amazed at your brightness.
You showed them then your light:
illuminate our souls.

On the mountain you were transfigured,
and as far as they could
your disciples, Christ our God,
saw your glory;
so that when they saw you crucified,
they might understand you suffered
of your own free will,
and might proclaim to the world
that you are indeed
the Father's reflection.

Word of God,
you are the unchanged light
of the unbegotten Father's light.
In your light,
displayed today on Tabor,

we have seen the Father as light,
and the Spirit as light,
who brings to the light
the whole of creation.

You are God the Word
from before all ages;
you wrap yourself in light
as with a garment.
When you were transfigured
in the presence of your disciples,
you shone, Word of God,
more brightly than the sun.
Moses and Elijah stood before you,
declaring you Lord
of dead and living.
They glorified your plan,
beyond human telling,
and your compassion
and your great self-abasement,
by which you have saved a world
lost because of sin.

The transfiguration of Jesus occurred soon after his prediction of his suffering and death. The disciples were naturally dismayed. The hymns for the feast present the transfiguration first of all as an anticipation of the resurrection, which was meant to encourage the disciples. But the light that shone from Jesus on Mount Tabor did not last, because Jesus could enter into the glory of the Father only by way of the cross. In the Gospel according to John the crucifixion of Jesus is at the same time his glorification; and after his death the light of his glory will shine permanently as the light of the resurrection.

Yet the resurrection itself is only a foretaste of the final glory, when Christ comes to establish the kingdom of God in power. So the light of Tabor is an anticipation too of the parousia, the final coming of the Lord in glory. Meanwhile, the presence and work of the Holy Spirit in the Church and in the world spreads the new life of the resurrection, which will come to full fruition in God's kingdom.

That kingdom is present even before his death in the person of Jesus, on whom the Spirit rested at his baptism; and the light that shone from him on Tabor is the light of the Holy Spirit. That light first of all reveals the divinity of Jesus, in whom, says St Paul, 'the whole fullness of deity dwells bodily' (Colossians 2.9). But, as the Council of Chalcedon affirmed, Jesus is not only perfect in his divinity: he is also perfect in his humanity. So the transfigured Jesus is also the revelation of what a human being, created in the image and likeness of God, is meant to be. In the Orthodox understanding of humanity, the Fall has not deprived us of the image of God, but it has taken away our likeness to him. That likeness is restored in Jesus, the proper man, as Luther called him.

The transfiguration of Jesus, like his baptism, is a revelation of the Trinity. Jesus, God the Son, the Second Person of the Trinity, shines with the light of the Holy Spirit, the Third Person of the Trinity; while the voice of the Father, the First Person, proclaims Jesus' Sonship. It is the light of the Trinity which dazzles the disciples' sight on the holy mountain, and causes them to fall to the ground in amazement.

The icon of the transfiguration reveals one further aspect of the meaning of the event. The light which streams from Jesus falls not only on the disciples; it illumines also the mountainside, representing the created order. In Orthodox thought the whole of the material creation is destined to be transformed in the kingdom of God. Orthodoxy does not separate the material and the spiritual. The material creation is meant to become the home of the Spirit and to find its fulfilment within the life of the Trinity.

The transfiguration of Jesus concerns therefore not only him personally, but ourselves and all creation. It is a sign of all humankind's eventual transfiguration, within a trans-formed universe. When we contemplate the icon of this feast, we contemplate our own ultimate destiny.

9 ASSUMPTION

The end of Mary's life, like its beginning, is described only in so-called apocryphal writings. Evidence of interest in her death appears first in the fourth century. The story may have originated in Egypt, but many versions of it circulated in various languages. Each differs in detail from the others. A Greek account, entitled *The Discourse of St John the Divine concerning the Falling Asleep of the Mother of God* tells how Mary used to go to her Son's sepulchre to burn incense, and ask him to come and abide with her. One day Gabriel came, and told her that, in response to her petition, she would soon leave the world and be brought to her Son in heaven. John and the rest of the apostles were brought miraculously to Mary's home in Bethlehem on clouds. Those who had died were raised up for the occasion. They explained to Mary, as she sat up in bed, how they had been summoned to her passing. Marvels took place in Bethlehem, as Mary's house was surrounded by an angelic host, and many were healed.

The apostles set out for Jerusalem, carrying Mary on her bed. The governor, at the urgent insistence of the Jews, sent soldiers to drive her away from Bethlehem and Jerusalem. But a cloud lifted up Mary and the apostles, and carried them to Mary's house in Jerusalem. Again, many signs and wonders took place, and a great crowd stood outside, beseeching Mary not to forget the human race. The Jews tried to set fire to the house, but were prevented by a rush of fire from within the house, which killed many of them.

One Sunday Christ appeared with a host of angels, and called to his Mother. She looked up and saw him in glory. She prayed, and blessed the apostles; and her soul was received by her Son's hands. Her body was laid on a bed and carried out. It was attacked by a Jew named Jephonias, but an angel cut off both his hands. He asked Mary for mercy, and at Peter's word his hands were joined back on.

The apostles laid Mary's body in a new tomb in Gethsemane. A sweet smell came out of the tomb, and for three days angelic voices were heard, praising Christ her Son. On the third day the voices ceased, and the apostles perceived that her body had been taken away to paradise. Then they beheld the choirs of the saints worshipping the body of the Lord's Mother, and saw a place of great light and fragrance to which her body had been carried. They glorified God for his wonders shown at Mary's departing.

In a Latin version the archangel Michael rolled away the stone from Mary's sepulchre, and in the presence of the apostles Christ called his mother, and she rose up from the grave. The Lord kissed her, and angels carried her away into paradise. In another Latin version Thomas, who had doubted the Lord's resurrection, was not present at Mary's burial. But he was brought from India to the Mount of Olives immediately after it, and saw her body being taken up to heaven by angels. Mary's girdle was thrown down to him. When the other apostles – who had not seen the body going to heaven – refused to believe the tomb was empty, Thomas told them what he had seen and showed them the girdle.

The imagery of the hymns for the Dormition, or Falling Asleep, of the Mother of God is drawn from this apocryphal literature. Their language reflects a theological tradition regarding Mary already well developed. Like the story of her birth and early life, the various writings in which this tradition was embodied served to promote an exalted view of Mary' significance and personal stature, which became an unquestioned part of the Church's tradition in both East and West until the Reformation.

The icon of the feast draws its imagery from the apocryphal story. It shows Mary lying on a bed, with the apostles, including Paul, at its head and foot. Behind is the figure of Christ in glory, holding a tiny figure wrapped in white, symbol of Mary's soul. Sometimes Jephonias is depicted, his hands cut off but still clinging to the edge of the bed.

Forefeast of the Dormition of the Mother of God

14 August

FROM VESPERS

Let us strike the cymbals,
and cry out in song,
as we begin to celebrate
the feast of her passing.
Let us sing songs
at her radiant grave.
For the Mother of God,
the golden ark,
prepares now to pass
from earth to heaven,
to the brightness of God
eternally dazzling.

Priests met together,
emperors and rulers,
with throngs of virgins,
prepare in advance;
you people, go with them
and all raise together
her burial song.
For the Lady of all
will tomorrow commit her soul
into her Son's hands,
passing to her eternal home.

The angelic hosts in heaven,
the human race on earth,
we bless your saintly sleeping,
most holy Virgin pure.
For you became Christ's Mother,
God and Creator of all.
Cease not to pray him for us,
who hope, after God, in you,
Mother of God most praised,
who has not known man.

She who is higher
than the heavens,
more glorious
than the cherubim,
held in more honour
than all creation,
whose great purity
made her fit
to be the dwelling
of eternal Being,
into her Son's hands
today commits her holy soul.
With her are all things
filled with joy,
and to us is given
abundant mercy.

FROM MATINS

The angelic hosts glorify you,
the human race sings your praise,
as we celebrate the forefeast.
For you have passed from earth
to him who was born of you,
pure Mother of God.

Now earnestly we pray you,
O Virgin, that we
who celebrate in faith
your falling asleep
may be saved from adversity.

Celebrating the forefeast
of God's Mother's passing,
radiant with joy,
let us cry out to her:
Greetings, for you have gone up
from earth to heaven!
Greetings, for you have raised up
the ends of the earth
by your falling asleep!
So now, passing on,
remember the world,
O Lady most favoured.

Now let heaven rejoice,
all creation leap for joy.
For the Virgin leaves earth,
and goes to paradise.
Praying and protecting, to all
she has shown God's salvation.
So the whole band of apostles
came swiftly together
from the ends of the earth.
For clouds appeared suddenly,
and bore them away;
and they stood in the presence
of Mother and Son,
and they cried out:
Greetings, treasure house
of the new covenant's manna!

Greetings, O Virgin,
Christians' boast!

Gloriously commemorating
your holy falling asleep,
we lovingly magnify you,
Mother of God.
And as you go,
most pure Mother,
in your glory
to your Son and Lord,
pray for the Christians
who praise you with faith.

Dormition of the Mother of God
15 August

FROM VESPERS

Amazing marvel!
Life's source
is laid in a tomb,
the tomb becomes
a ladder up to heaven.
Rejoice, Gethsemane,
sacred precinct
of God's Mother.
We who believe,
led by Gabriel,
cry we out:
Greetings, favoured one!
the Lord is with you;
through you he grants
to the world great mercy.

It was fitting
that the eye-witnesses
and servants of the Word
should see too his Mother's
falling asleep in the body,
the final mystery in her regard:
that they might see not only
the Saviour's ascension,
but be also witnesses
of her passing,
who gave him birth.
So, by God's power
brought together
from every place,
they came to Sion,
and sent on her way
to heaven the one
who is exalted above the cherubim.
We too with them venerate her,
who prays for us.

The blameless bride and Mother
of him in whom the Father
was well pleased,
predestined by God
as the dwelling of him
who is one person in two natures,
human and divine,
today commends her spotless soul
to her Creator and God.
The angelic powers welcome her
with divine honours;
and there passes over into life
the one who is indeed Life's Mother,
unapproachable Light's torch,

believers' salvation,
and our souls' hope.

David's song sing we
today, O people,
to Christ our God,
for he says:
The virgins who follow her,
shall be brought to the king,
they shall be led
with joy and gladness.
For she who is of David's line,
through whom we have been deified,
commits herself into the hands
of her Son and Master
in manner glorious
and beyond all telling.
We praise her as God's Mother,
and calling out we say:
Save us, who acknowledge you,
from every menace, God's Birthgiver,
and rescue us from every danger.

FROM MATINS

When you gave birth,
you conceived without seed;
when you fell asleep,
death brought no decay.
The second miracle, Mother of God,
followed hard on the first.
For how could one
who knew no man
give suck, remaining pure?
How could God's Mother
suffer death,

yet give out fragrance?
So we cry out with the angel:
Greetings, favoured one!

When the passing
of your undefiled body
was in preparation,
the Apostles, standing round your bed
looked upon you, trembling with fear.
Some were seized with awe,
as they fixed their eyes
on your earthly tabernacle.
Tearfully Peter cried out to you:
O Virgin, clearly I see you
stretched out on a bed,
you, the life of all,
and I am amazed.
For in you dwelt the delight
of the life that shall be.
But, most pure Lady,
earnestly entreat
your Son and God
to preserve your city* unharmed.

You conquered nature,
Virgin pure,
in giving birth to God;
beyond nature's ways,
like your Son and maker,
you bowed to nature's laws;
and so you rose by dying,
with your Son eternally alive.

If the fruit of her womb,
whom nothing can bound,

* i.e., Constantinople

for whose sake
she was named heaven,
as mortal man
suffered willing tomb,
how could she refuse a tomb,
who bore him,
yet knew not a man?

Apostles, gathered here
from the ends of the earth,
bury my body
in Gethsemane's field;
and you, my Son and God,
receive my spirit.

From the ends of the earth
the chosen of the apostles,
by God's command,
came to bury you.
When they saw you
lifted from earth
and raised to heaven,
they joyfully cried out
with Gabriel's voice:
Greetings, entire
Divinity's vessel!
Greetings, for by giving birth
you alone have gathered into one
all things earthly and heavenly!

In later Western tradition, officially defined by Rome in 1950, Mary was assumed body and soul into heaven. In Eastern Christian tradition Mary died and was buried, and at her death her soul was taken into heaven. Her body was raised on the third day. In Jerusalem Mary's tomb is next to Gethsemane.

The celebration of the Falling Asleep of the Mother of God in Jerusalem is modelled on that of the death, burial and resurrection of her Son. On 13 August her death is commemorated. A procession makes its way from a place near the Church of the Resurrection, or Holy Sepulchre, along the Via Dolorosa and out of the Old City, down to the Tomb of Mary in the Kedron Valley. At the head of the procession is carried an image of Mary's dead body. The image is taken down into the sepulchre, and laid on the tomb. Then on 15 August is celebrated the translation of her body to heaven, her resurrection.

This liturgical celebration, derived entirely from the apocryphal tradition, can nevertheless be given positive theological significance in the light of basic Christian faith. Mary's Son walked up the Via Dolorosa; he carried his cross, going from life to death. But by his death he frees us from the power of death, and gives us new life. Mary is carried down the Via Dolorosa; she goes from death to life, the first, according to tradition, to receive the gift of new and eternal life from her Son.

The transfiguration of Jesus does not concern him alone, but points to the ultimate transformation of all creation. In the same way the dormition of the Mother of God is not about her entry into glory alone, but shows us the destiny God intends for the whole human race. The divine plan of salvation, whose first beginnings we have seen in the birth of the Virgin, has now come to fruition in her passing from death to life. If the risen Christ is 'the first fruits of those who have died' (1 Corinthians 15.20), Mary is the first who has been 'made alive in Christ' (1 Corinthians 15.22). So we can understand her entry into glory as the pledge of our own participation in the eternal life won for us by the death and resurrection of Jesus Christ. It is the pledge, too, of the healing of all creation, destined to be transfigured by the creative and redemptive suffering love of God in Christ.

Taken together, the two feasts of the Transfiguration and

the Dormition can be seen as celebrating St Paul's hope that 'the creation itself will be set free from its bondage to decay and obtain the glorious liberty of the children of God' (Romans 8.21). Paul's words are in the future tense. But the icons of these feasts make present realities of what they depict in images. For in the Spirit it is possible to experience now the first-fruits of God's redeeming work. That salvation will be revealed in its fullness when God brings to completion what he has begun in the birth, life, death and resurrection of Jesus Christ, born of the Virgin Mary, fully human and truly divine.

Already 'my beloved is mine, and I am his'. But there is far more to come. John wrote in his first letter, 'Beloved, we are God's children now; what we will be has not yet been revealed. What we do know is this: when he is revealed, we will be like him, for we shall see him as he is. And all who have this hope in him purify themselves, just as he is pure' (1 John 3.2–3).

*

Amen. Come, Lord Jesus!

BIBLIOGRAPHY

The Festal Menaion, translated from the original Greek by Mother Mary and Archimandrite Kallistos Ware. London, Faber & Faber, 1969.

The Apocryphal New Testament, edited by J. K. Elliott. Oxford, Clarendon Press, 1993.

The Origins of the Liturgical Year, by Thomas J. Talley. New York, Pueblo Publishing Company, 1986.

The Society for Promoting Christian Knowledge (SPCK) has as its purpose three main tasks:

- **Communicating the Christian faith in its rich diversity**
- **Helping people to understand the Christian faith and to develop their personal faith**
- **Equipping Christians for mission and ministry**

SPCK Worldwide serves the Church through Christian literature and communication projects in over 100 countries. Special schemes also provide books for those training for ministry in many parts of the developing world. SPCK Worldwide's ministry involves Churches of many traditions. This worldwide service depends upon the generosity of others and all gifts are spent wholly on ministry programmes, without deductions.

SPCK Bookshops support the life of the Christian community by making available a full range of Christian literature and other resources, and by providing support to bookstalls and book agents throughout the UK. SPCK Bookshops' mail order department meets the needs of overseas customers and those unable to have access to local bookshops.

SPCK Publishing produces Christian books and resources, covering a wide range of inspirational, pastoral, practical and academic subjects. Authors are drawn from many different Christian traditions, and publications aim to meet the needs of a wide variety of readers in the UK and throughout the world.

The Society does not necessarily endorse the individual views contained in its publications, but hopes they stimulate readers to think about and further develop their Christian faith.

For further information about the Society, please write to:
SPCK, Holy Trinity Church, Marylebone Road,
London NW1 4DU, United Kingdom.
Telephone: 0171 387 5282